Youth in the MENA Region

HOW TO BRING THEM IN

Please cite this publication as:
OECD (2016), *Youth in the MENA Region: How to Bring Them In*, OECD Publishing, Paris.
http://dx.doi.org/10.1787/9789264265721-en

ISBN 978-92-64-26573-8 (print)
ISBN 978-92-64-26572-1 (PDF)

Photo credits: Cover © John Lund/Blend Images/Getty Images.

Corrigenda to OECD publications may be found on line at: *www.oecd.org/about/publishing/corrigenda.htm*.

Foreword

Young men and women in the Middle East and North Africa (MENA) region face the highest youth unemployment levels in the world and express lower levels of trust in government than their parents. With the share of youth (aged 15-29) exceeding 30% of the working-age population in most countries, MENA countries need to urgently develop and implement strategies focused on fully engaging youth in the economy, society and public life. So far, young people have only limited opportunities to influence policy making, and many lack adequate access to decent employment, quality education and affordable healthcare. The report is the first of its kind to apply a "youth lens" to public governance arrangements. It argues that governments can use open government tools to foster inclusive policy-making with a view to raising their voice in shaping policies and involving them in governance processes such as the allocation of public budgets. By "bringing youth in" to the policy-making process governments help ensure that their needs and concerns are taken into account across the whole of government. With youth on board, governments are more likely to deliver public services that are tailored to their specific needs and more accessible for vulnerable sub-groups such as young women and youth from rural backgrounds.

Based on comparative data from seven MENA countries (Egypt, Jordan, Libya, Morocco, the Palestinian Authority, Tunisia and Yemen), the report presents good practices from OECD and MENA countries and policy recommendations to make youth a partner of government across the policy cycle.

This report supports the work on youth in the MENA-OECD Governance Programme which has systematically embraced and mainstreamed youth issues in its activities during 2016-2020. The report also contributes to OECD-wide work on the critical role of collaborative and participatory governance for inclusive growth, in line with the OECD Action Plan on Youth, the OECD New Approaches to Economic Challenges (NAEC) initiative, the OECD report *Policy Shaping and Policy Making: The Governance of Inclusive Growth*, the OECD Open Government Project and the OECD Guiding Principles for Open and Inclusive Policy Making. The report is complemented by the paper "Tackling youth unemployment in the MENA region" by the MENA-OECD Competitiveness Programme, which discusses strategies to encourage young people's economic inclusion.

Following informal presentations of the report in the 9th UNESCO Youth Forum on 26-28 October 2015 in Paris and the "Youth Dialogue for Inclusive Growth" with youth representatives and ministers from OECD and MENA countries on 27 October 2015 in Helsinki, a preliminary version of the report was presented during the Steering Group Meeting of the MENA-OECD Initiative on 9 November 2015 in Rabat, Morocco.

The final report was launched by the co-chairs of the MENA-OECD Governance Programme, Ambassador José Ignacio Wert, Permanent Representative of Spain to the OECD, and Kamel Ayadi, Minister of Civil Service, Governance and Fight Against Corruption in Tunisia, on 18 April 2016 in Paris.

Acknowledgements

This report was prepared by the MENA-OECD Governance Programme, Governance Reviews and Partnerships Division in the OECD Directorate for Public Governance and Territorial Development (GOV).

The OECD Secretariat wishes to express its gratitude to all stakeholders who provided valuable information and feedback throughout the drafting process. The Secretariat acknowledges the significant contributions and strategic guidance provided by the participants of the break-out session, "Citizen participation: Engaging the Youth" in the framework of the OECD International Forum on Open Government on 30 September 2014 in Paris, the participants of the OECD Idea Factory "Inclusive Policies for Young Men and Women in MENA" on 4 February 2015 in Paris, organised jointly with the MENA-OECD Competitiveness Programme and the participation of the OECD Directorate for Employment, Labour and Social Affairs, as well as the youth associations and civil society representatives attending the seminar "Impliquer la société marocaine pour le gouvernement ouvert: Élargir la participation de la société civile au processes de l'OGP au Maroc" and from delegates of the various regional networks of the MENA-OECD Governance Programme. The Secretariat is grateful for the feedback received during a strategic discussion of the report with members of the MENA-OECD Civil Society Advisory Board on 29 September 2015 in Rabat.

This report was produced under the leadership of Rolf Alter, Director of the Public Governance and Territorial Development Directorate and Martin Forst, Head of Governance Reviews and Partnerships Division and the supervision of Miriam Allam, Head of the MENA-Governance Programme. The report was drafted by Moritz Ader with contributions from Jennifer Bremer. Alessandro Bellantoni provided strategic guidance and alignment with the OECD Open Government Project. The report received valuable comments by Adam Ostry, Paqui Santonja, Amira Tlili, and Katharina Zügel as well as feedback provided by Marco Daglio, Laura Skoratko, Guillaume Lafortune, Ronnie Downes and Faisal Naru. The report benefitted from discussions with Alexandre Kolev, Ji-Yeun Rim and Ian Brand-Weiner from the Youth Inclusion Project at the OECD Development Centre. The final editing and layout of the text was carried out by Julie Harris and Ciara Muller. The OECD Secretariat wishes to thank the United States, and in particular the Middle East Partnership Initiative (MEPI), Spain (AECID) and Turkey for the financial support of the regional programme activities of the MENA-OECD Governance Programme.

Table of contents

Tables

Figures

Acronyms and abbreviations

AECID	Spanish Agency for International Development Cooperation
CAPMAS	Central Agency for Public Mobilisation and Statistics (Arab Republic of Egypt)
CAWTAR	Centre for Arab Women for Training & Research
CiNI	Children in Northern Ireland
DCYA	Department of Children and Youth Affairs (Republic of Ireland)
EGDI	E-Government Development Index
ERYICA	European Youth Information and Counselling Agency
EYC	European Youth Capital
GCC	Gulf Co-operation Council
GDP	Gross Domestic Product
GOV	Public Governance and Territorial Development Directorate
HRM	Human Resource Management
ICAC	Independent Commission against Corruption
ICT	Information and Communications Technology
ILO	International Labour Organisation
IMF	International Monetary Fund
ITU	International Telecommunication Union
LiJOT	Lithuania Youth Council
LOLF	Organic Finance Law (*Loi Organique relative à la loi de finances*)
MENA	Middle East and North Africa
MEPI	Middle East Partnership Initiative
NAEC	New Approaches to Economic Challenges
NGO	Non-Governmental Organisation
NYC	National Youth Council
NEET	Not in Education, Employment or Training
OECD	Organisation for Economic Co-operation and Development
OGP	Open Government Partnership
RIA	Regulatory Impact Analysis
ROB	Result-Oriented Budgeting
SIDA	Swedish International Development Co-operation Agency
SOE	State-Owned Enterprise
SYPE	Survey of Young People in Egypt
TUNEPS	Tunisia's online e-procurement system
UTOJ	Tunisian Union of Youth Organisations
UNDP	United Nations Development Programme
UNHCR	United Nations High Commissioner for Refugees
UNICEF	United Nations Children's Fund
WoG	Whole-of-Government Approach
WPAY	World Programme of Action for Youth

Executive summary

Five years after what has become known as the Arab Spring, young men and women in the Middle East and North Africa (MENA) region still face considerable obstacles in becoming a driving force for social and economic development in their countries. MENA youth are facing higher unemployment levels than young people in any other region in the world. While around 15% of young people aged 15-29 in OECD countries as a whole are not in education, employment or training, inactivity levels for the age cohort 15-24 are as high as 25% for young men in the Palestinian Authority and around 41% for young women in Egypt. As the share of 15-29-year-olds exceeds 30% of the working-age population in most MENA countries, there is an urgent need to create decent opportunities for youth in both public and private sector to play a productive role in all areas of life, in particular by creating the space for youth to raise their voice and shape policies that reflect their realities and aspirations.

In the absence of inclusive institutions supporting dialogue and change, traditional forms of political engagement do not attract a significant share of young people, largely because these are dominated by older people and rigid structures discouraging young people to get involved. Contrary to the popular belief that young people are not interested in politics, recent evidence shows that a majority of MENA youth not only express a general interest in politics but are looking for ways to engage. While not all the youth-led civil society organisations that emerged during the political transformations in some MENA countries still exist, many have been successful as watchdogs, holding government accountable and offering new channels for young people to make themselves heard. Some countries have made efforts to create or strengthen youth representative bodies, such as national and local youth councils. However, there remain many untapped opportunities, such as innovative forms provided by digital technologies.

In line with global trends, some MENA countries are currently formulating or implementing integrated national youth policies cutting across different policy domains. By involving youth in the formulation, implementation and monitoring of a holistic youth strategy, governments can ensure that programmes and services respond to their needs. In previous efforts, however, lack of clarity in responsibilities, limited capacities for co-ordination and the absence of effective accountability mechanisms made implementation difficult.

As of today, results from the World Gallup Survey suggest that young people are dissatisfied with the performance of government in the MENA region. While young people in OECD countries express greater trust in government than their parents, albeit at a very low level, MENA youth have less confidence in their political representatives than the older generation. For MENA youth to become a driving force for and beneficiary of more inclusive growth, exclusive governance arrangements need to be tackled decisively to adjust the existing legislative, institutional and policy frameworks towards their ideas, needs and concerns.

Using open government tools to engage youth

In line with the efforts undertaken to render policy making more inclusive and informed, for instance through the Open Government Partnership, MENA governments could use open government tools such as access to information, citizen engagement and digital technologies to promote youth engagement. Access to information frameworks increases transparency, and can empower youth to participate and scrutinise government action. The availability of youth-disaggregated and integrated data is also critical for targeting youth-specific challenges in a holistic way. Governments could work with youth associations, civil society organisations and activists to formulate national youth policies. Creating or strengthening the role of youth representative bodies contributes to the emergence of more inclusive institutions to make young people's voices heard. Finally, young people increasingly grow up as "digital natives", and web-based consultation methods, social media and online public services could be used more effectively to engage them.

Involving youth in public governance processes

In their role as students, workers, customers or voters, youth present a vulnerable target for corruption and undue influence. Governments could strengthen integrity frameworks in partnership with youth, media and independent institutions, for example by raising the awareness of integrity standards among young people, and engaging them in monitoring the implementation of policies and programmes and reporting corruption.

The public budget is a powerful instrument for turning national strategies into reality, and election pledges into tangible improvements. Governments can engage youth in the strategic allocation of public expenditures, for example by publishing a "Citizen's Budget" highlighting youth-related expenditures, using participatory budgeting approaches, and improving young people's financial literacy.

Public sectors in MENA countries, unable to formally hire any more skilled graduates, are increasingly resorting to informal employment. Furthermore, they often lack good human resources management (HR) practices. To address these challenges, governments could reinforce standardised and merit-based recruitment and promotion, monitor contract-based hiring, and introduce better HR resource planning and management as well as placement systems in schools to help students enter the job market.

MENA countries could take a more inclusive and youth-sensitive approach to regulatory policy. For example, regulatory impact assessments and cost-benefit-analysis could help governments anticipate the share of costs and benefits among different segments of society, including youth and relevant sub-groups. In addition, reviewing the stock of existing legislation could help foster an economic environment encouraging business activity, youth entrepreneurship and job creation.

Local youth councils can help identify needs and hold authorities to account. Young people could also be encouraged to volunteer and participate in the development of their municipality or neighbourhood. Governments should work with local universities and technical institutes to help youth acquire job-relevant skills.

Young women often confront a double challenge of both gender-based and youth-based barriers. To address this double challenge, governments could undertake a systematic review of legislation to eliminate all forms of discrimination, in particular those affecting young women; elimination provisions in workplace regulation that discourage young women to apply for jobs; integrate the demands of young women in national youth strategies and gender equality strategies; gather sex- and age-disaggregated data sets to promote better informed policy decisions; and increase the opportunities for young women and women associations to participate in all spheres of public life.

Chapter 1

Readjusting public governance frameworks towards youth demands and inclusive growth

Despite the prominent role they played in the civil uprisings in the early 2010s, MENA youth are trapped in an observer status. Five years after young men and women took to the streets to call for more democratic governance and economic opportunities, they are facing limited opportunities to influence policy making. Moreover, access to decent employment, quality education and affordable healthcare is restricted for many. With the serious deterioration of the security situation in some countries, a whole generation of young men and women is facing the risk of social and economic exclusion. In line with the OECD New Approaches to Economic Challenges (NAEC) initiative, the OECD report, "Policy Shaping and Policy Making: The Governance of Inclusive Growth" as well as the OECD Guiding Principles for Open and Inclusive Policy Making, this chapter introduces the argument that MENA governments need to readjust their public governance arrangements towards the demands of young people to make inclusive growth happen and deliver tailored public services.

A popular narrative says youth are the future. In light of the demographics and the massive challenges faced by young men and women in the Middle East and North Africa (MENA) region, this storyline must change. With a staggering share of 70% of the Jordanian population under the age of 30, for instance, policies in favour of youth are not only an investment in the future but in the well-being of today's population.

In most countries in the MENA region, youth[1] make up more than a quarter of the population, with growing demographic pressure and unemployment rates exceeding those in all other regions of the world (Assaad and Levison, 2013). Young people's exclusion from a fair share of the economic progress over recent decades has produced a pattern of rising income inequality. Worrying figures from OECD countries show that income inequality has translated into higher poverty rates with a shift in the age profile of the poor, with children and youth being particularly vulnerable to increasing poverty rates (OECD, 2016a). The absence of effective public institutions to represent youth needs and youth-tailored strategies has left young men and women at the margin of society with restricted access to social safety and limited access to public services of good quality.

Despite average annual growth rates in real gross domestic product (GDP) of almost 5% in MENA countries between 2000 and 2010, the economic upswing did not translate into increased job creation and economic opportunities (IMF, 2015).[2] Instead, over the last few years, youth unemployment rates have skyrocketed up to 51% in Libya, 39% in Egypt and 38% in the Palestinian Authority (World Bank, 2016). While young people feel that living costs are on a steady rise, wages stagnate. Youth inactivity in terms of the share of young people not in education, employment or training (NEET) is nowhere higher than in the Middle East and North Africa, especially among young women (Yassin, 2014). This pattern presents a significant risk of excluding youth and in particular young women from full participation in public life as recognised by the OECD Recommendation on Gender Equality in Public Life. Despite improvements in the access to higher education, more than 30% in Morocco and more than 50% of all youth in Yemen are not enrolled in secondary education. The failure of government to deliver quality services across all segments and age groups of society comes at high social costs. It risks pulling apart the social cohesion and erodes trust in the state as a steward of youth interests. Indeed, youth in the MENA countries covered in this report unanimously report lower levels of trust in government than the age group of 50+ (see Chapter 3).

Young people in the MENA region are subject to a highly volatile political environment and external shocks. Following the serious deterioration of the security situation in Syria, Yemen, Libya and other countries, many have been forced to flee their homes. In Yemen, as of end 2015, for instance, the United Nations High Commissioner for Refugees (UNHCR) estimates that around 170 000 individuals have fled to neighbouring countries and that about 2.5 million people were internally displaced during 2015 (UNHCR, 2016). Considering that half of the Yemini population was under the age of 19, an entire new generation risks growing up in an environment of armed conflict. Countries hosting large refugee communities such as Jordan and Lebanon face the challenge of providing basic access to education and health services in a context in which capacities are already scarce.

OECD evidence suggests that public governance matters for breaking down the barriers to inclusive growth which it defines as "economic growth that creates opportunity for all segments of the population and distributes the dividends of increased prosperity, both in monetary and non-monetary terms, fairly across society" (OECD, 2015a). The role of public governance – the system of strategic processes and tools, as well as institutions, rules and interactions for effective policy making – has been recognised in the OECD New Approaches to Economic Challenges (NAEC) initiative and the OECD report, *Policy Shaping and Policy Making: The Governance of Inclusive Growth* (OECD, 2016a). It argues that public sector strategies, tools and processes should be aligned towards inclusive growth outcomes across the policy-making cycle (*policy making*) based on a more inclusive process of identifying policy challenges and implementation (*policy shaping*).

For young men and women in the MENA region to become a driving force and beneficiary of more inclusive growth, governments need to readjust existing public governance arrangements. With a view to the arrangements in place, youth are suffering from a two-fold marginalisation.[3] Young people play a marginal role in shaping policies. In a context in which their voice in the public discourse is silent and access to the critical stages of the decision-making process is blocked, they are unlikely to become a source of creativity and scrutiny. Despite the fact that students were among the most active drivers of the civil uprisings in the MENA region, calling for more transparent, inclusive and accountable governments, opportunities for youth associations and activists to influence policy outcomes still remain fairly limited.

Moreover, youth considerations in public policies and strategies are largely absent. As a multi-dimensional field of public policy, youth considerations should be mainstreamed and co-ordinated across various ministries and departments (e.g. employment, education, health, family, women, culture, and sports). A whole-of-government (WoG) approach to youth policy can break down silo-based approaches and deliver youth-dedicated policies and services in a coherent manner both horizontally and vertically across government, for instance in the form of a national youth policy. In turn, when youth considerations are mainstreamed across departments and government agencies, sectoral policy frameworks are flexible enough to internalise the specific needs of youth. The current fragmented approach tends to favour narrow initiatives at the expense of the coherent deliver of pro-youth policies and services.

In recent years, the attention of policy makers and international organisations has been directed towards training youth to increase their skills and facilitate their integration into the labour market. The OECD Action Plan for Youth aims at giving youth a better start in the labour market by tackling the youth unemployment crisis and strengthening young people's long-term employment prospects. The Action Plan is complemented by a forward-looking skills strategy, measures to promote youth entrepreneurship and financial education tailored at the younger cohorts (OECD, 2016b). Recent publications follow this trend. The report *Investing in Youth: Tunisia* (OECD, 2015b) looks at ways to strengthen the employability of youth during the transition to a green economy. "NEET youth in the aftermath of the crisis" (Carcillo et al., 2015) also describes the characteristics and living conditions of youth not in employment, education or training. The paper "Tackling youth unemployment in the MENA region" by the MENA-OECD Competitiveness Programme (OECD, 2015c) discusses government strategies to promote economic inclusion by creating decent, well-paying and secure jobs for youth.

The OECD Youth Dialogue on 27 October 2015 in Helsinki shed light on the importance of making young people's voices heard in political decision-making processes. With Ministers from OECD and MENA countries, youth representatives were given the opportunity to discuss policy solutions that matter for building stronger, fairer and more inclusive societies. However, despite an increasing awareness of the importance of giving young people an active stake in shaping policy debates, only a handful of papers explores the connections between good public governance, youth engagement and youth-tailored policy outcomes. These papers provide useful insights into the governance parameters to foster their engagement, however, they typically apply a narrow focus, such as the civic engagement of youth (Mercy Corps, 2012).

This report aims to close that gap. Against the background of the two-fold challenge outlined above – the exclusion of young people from the policy cycle and the lack of mainstreamed youth concerns in public policies and strategies – this report outlines pathways for governments to "bring them in". By "bringing youth in", this report understands that governments provide systematic opportunities for youth from all backgrounds to shape the policy agenda with effective mechanisms in place to hold policy makers accountable. In light of the limited opportunities for today's youth to access the political arena, it suggests that policy makers should apply a "youth lens" to open government[4] tools and traditional forms of policy making. With OECD support, some MENA countries have started to encourage openness, transparency, accountability and more participatory approaches through the Open Government Partnership. By applying a youth lens to open government tools, MENA governments could direct their focus from a rather abstract notion of "citizens" as a target group to an immediate beneficiary (and potential contributor to the elaboration and implementation) of public policies and services.

Moreover, a whole-of-government approach[5] to steer youth policy across different departments and agencies should build on a shared perception that governance matters. It requires a new understanding that youth can play a productive role in governance processes and areas that have been left at the discretion of policy makers, including in purportedly technical areas such as the allocation of public expenditures. Bringing pro-youth perspectives into the mainstream of government activities requires strong political will and a long-term commitment to overcome piecemeal reform and short-term responses.

Notes

1. This report will use the United Nations definition of "youth" as those between 15 and 24 years of age. For some purposes, particularly the analysis of the school-to-work transition, this age range may be extended to include young people between 24 and 29.

2. The GDP growth rate refers to the average of the countries covered in this study except for the Palestinian Authority for which no data was available.

3. In line with the definition in provided by the OECD report (2016a), *Policy Shaping and Policy Making: The Governance of Inclusive Growth*, this report understands public governance as the "strategic processes and tools, as well as institutions, rules and interactions for effective policy making."

4. The OECD defines open government as: "The transparency of government actions, the accessibility of government services and information, and the responsiveness of government to new ideas, demands and needs" (OECD, 2005).

5. This approach can in many ways build on the established principles and experience of gender-responsive programming and public governance reform. Indeed, gender-responsive programming and pro-youth programming share many features, not only because half of youth are women, but because youth and women alike too often suffer from exclusion, inadequate public services, and limited opportunities for participation, not only in governance but also in local development and the national economy.

References

Assaad, Ragui and Deborah Levison (2013), "Employment for youth–A growing challenge for the global economy," background research paper submitted to the High Level Panel on the Post-2015 Development Agenda, May.

Carcillo, S., et al. (2015), "NEET youth in the aftermath of the crisis: Challenges and policies", *OECD Social, Employment and Migration Working Papers*, No. 164, OECD Publishing, http://dx.doi.org/10.1787/5js6363503f6-en.

IMF (International Monetary Fund) (2015), *IMF World Economic Outlook Database,* www.imf.org/external/pubs/ft/weo/2015/02/weodata/index.aspx (accessed on 12 April 2016).

Mercy Corps (2012), "Civic engagement of youth in the Middle East and North Africa: An analysis of key drivers and outcomes", March, www.mercycorps.org/sites/default/files/mena_youth_civic_engagement_study_-_final.pdf (accessed on 1 April 2016).

OECD (2016a), *Policy Shaping and Policy Making: The Governance of Inclusive Growth,* www.oecd.org/governance/ministerial/the-governance-of-inclusive-growth.pdf (accessed on 10 April 2016).

OECD (2016b), "OECD work on Youth", www.oecd.org/employment/youth.htm (accessed on 1 April 2016).

OECD (2015a), *All on Board: Making Inclusive Growth Happen,* OECD Publishing, Paris, http://dx.doi.org/10.1787/9789264218512-en.

OECD (2015b), *Investing in Youth: Tunisia: Strengthening the Employability of Youth during the Transition to a Green Economy,* OECD Publishing, Paris, http://dx.doi.org/10.1787/9789264226470-en.

OECD (2015c), "Tackling youth unemployment in the MENA region", key findings in the presentation, "Idea Factory on inclusive policies for young men and women in MENA", www.oecd.org/mena/investment/PPT_website.pdf (accessed on 2 April 2016).

OECD (2005), "Open Government", in *Modernising Government: The Way Forward,* OECD Publishing, Paris, http://dx.doi.org/10.1787/9789264010505-en.

UNHCR (United Nations High Commissioner for Refugees) (2016), "Global trends - Forced displacement in 2015", www.unhcr.org/576408cd7.pdf (accessed on 1 April 2016).

World Bank (2016), "Unemployment, youth total (percent of total labour force ages 15-24)", modeled ILO estimate, http://data.worldbank.org/indicator/SL.UEM.1524.ZS (accessed on 1 April 2016).

Yassin, Sabha (2014), "Youth employment in Egypt and Tunisia vs. Jordan and Morocco – Three years after the Arab Awakening", *World Bank News*, http://blogs.worldbank.org/arabvoices/youth-employment-egypt-and-tunisia-vs-jordan-and-morocco-three-years-after-arab-awakening (accessed on 10 April 2016).

Chapter 2

A glance at youth in the MENA region

This chapter takes a snapshot of the conditions for MENA youth to shape their future. It finds that the region's largest youth cohort of all times is unsatisfied with the delivery of public services and policies that do not adequately address their needs. Today, exclusive public governance arrangements present a major impediment, which, in the case they remain unaddressed, risk slowing down young people's transition to adulthood and active citizenship. With unemployment levels exceeding 30% in most countries and an even greater share of discouraged young men and women not in employment, education or training (NEET), MENA countries are deprived of a key source for their future social and economic development. Low levels of traditional forms of participation suggest that MENA youth are disappointed with the existing mechanisms to drive change.

Young men and women in the Middle East and North Africa (MENA) region face considerable obstacles to participate in public, social and economic life. While some of these impediments are unique to the MENA region, others occur in the context of global transitions affecting the younger generation world wide (e.g. urbanisation; individualisation; knowledge society; digital media; increasing mobility). In principle, these transitions offer great opportunities to advance youth interests, in the absence of an enabling environment, however, youth are likely to be among the first who will be left behind.

Youth population and demographic development

This report will use the United Nations definition of "youth" covering those between 15 and 24 years of age. For some purposes, particularly the analysis of the school-to-work transition, this age range may be extended to include the 24-29 age group.

Table 2.1 presents the estimated youth population in the MENA countries involved in this study. It illustrates that the youth population in Egypt, Jordan, Libya, Morocco, the Palestinian Authority, Tunisia, and Yemen exceeds 32 million using the 15-24 years of age definition. Under the broader definition, the population approaches 48 million. The table further shows that the youth shares in MENA countries are typically higher than the global averages, both as share among the total population and the working-age population. For instance, Yemen and the Palestinian Authority have much higher youth shares in the latter category, with more than 26% of the working-age population between the ages of 15 and 24, compared to a global average of 19%. Using the broader definition, young men and women present almost one-third of the working-age population in MENA countries.

Table 2.1. **The youth population in selected MENA countries, 2015**

Major area, region, country or area	Population in millions		Share of working-age population (15-64, %)		Share of total population (%)	
	15-24	15-29	15-24	15-29	15-24	15-29
Egypt	15.04	22.76	20.7	31.3	13.5	20.5
Libya	1.06	1.61	19.5	29.4	13.0	19.7
Morocco	6.03	8.94	19.8	29.4	13.5	20.1
Tunisia	1.77	2.78	17.5	27.5	12.3	19.3
Jordan	1.43	2.12	21.5	31.9	14.0	20.8
Palestinian Authority	1.02	1.38	26.3	35.8	16.2	22.0
Yemen	5.80	8.14	26.5	37.2	16.4	22.9
Total, study countries	32.15	47.73	21.3	31.6	14.0	20.7
World	1 190 548	1 803 003	18.7	28.4	13.4	20.3

Source: United Nations (2013), *World Population Prospects: The 2012 Revision*, Department of Economic and Social Affairs, Population Division, DVD edition.

Figure 2.1 brings together the population pyramids for 1950, 2010 and 2050 projections. It illustrates that all study countries have experienced rapid population growth since 1950. Some countries are projected to see continued high rates of demographic expansion in the coming decades.

Figure 2.1. **Population pyramids for selected MENA countries, 1950, 2010, and 2050**

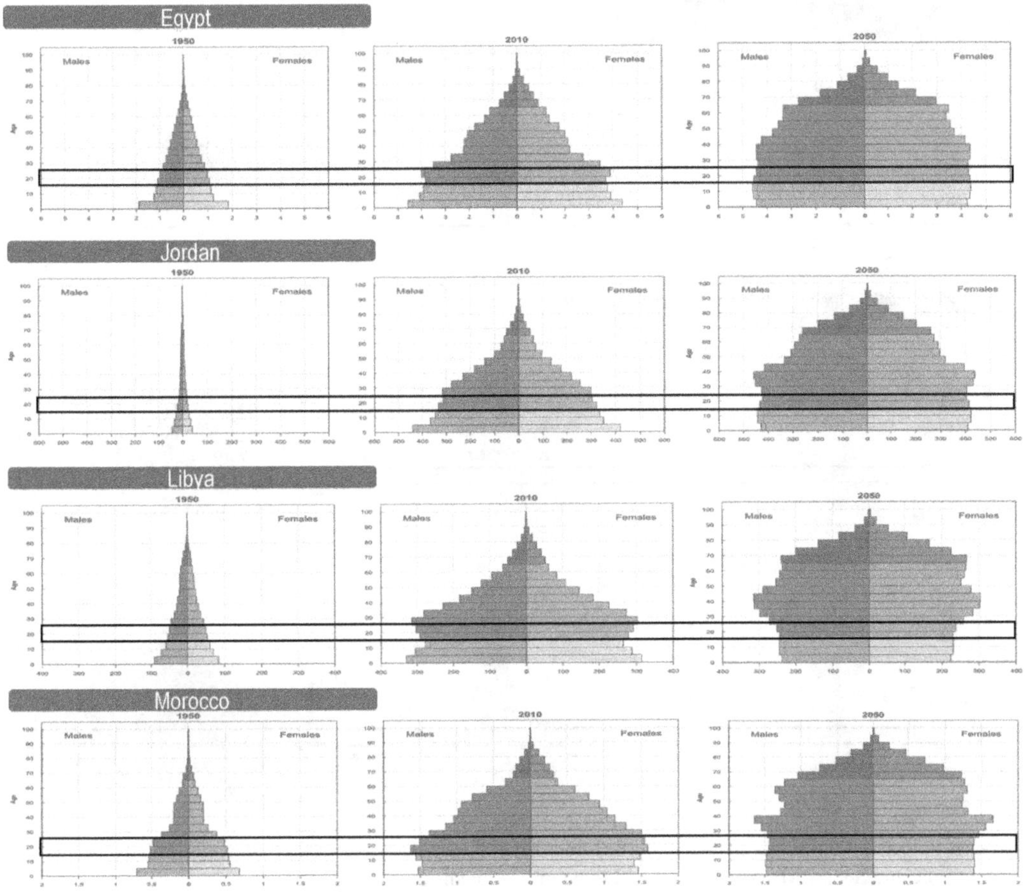
Egypt
1950
Males
Females
2010
Males
Females
2050
Males
Females
Jordan
1950
Males
Females
2010
Males
Females
2050
Males
Females
Libya
1950
Males
Females
2010
Males
Females
2050
Males
Females
Morocco
1950
Males
Females
2010
Males
Females
2050
Males
Females

Figure 2.1. **Population pyramids for selected MENA countries, 1950, 2010, and 2050** *(continued)*

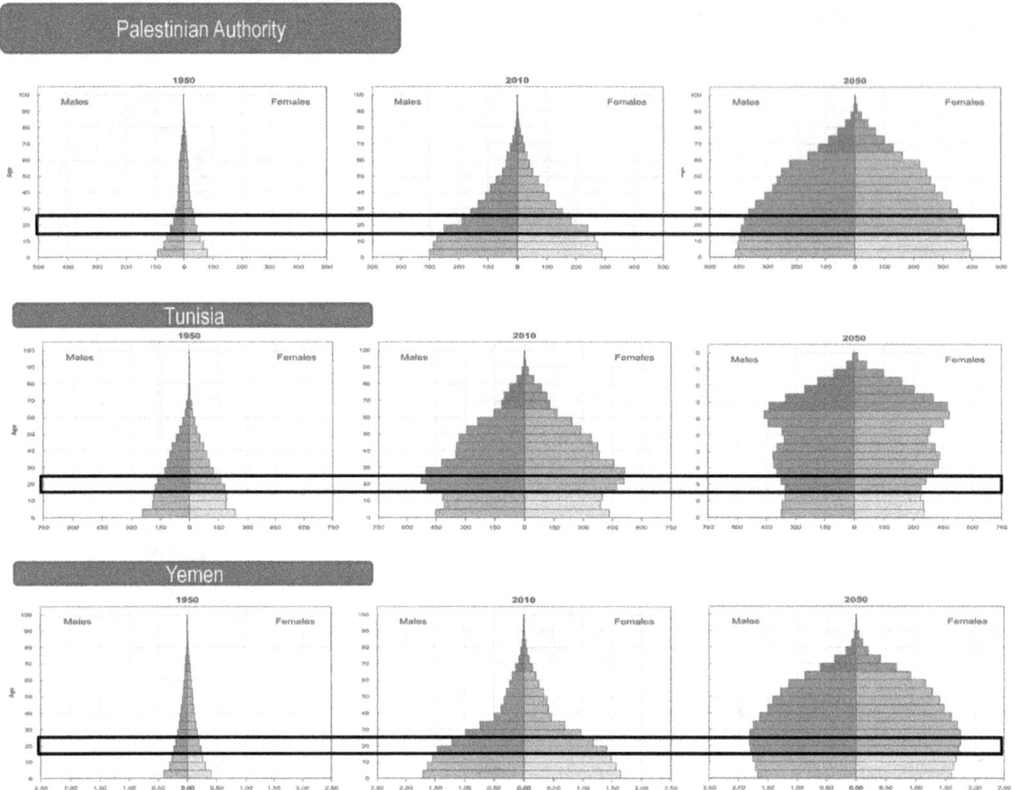

Source: United Nations (2013), *World Population Prospects: The 2012 Revision*, Department of Economic and Social Affairs, Population Division, DVD edition.

In OECD countries, rapid demographic changes have required an adaptation of government institutions and processes. The demographic situation in the MENA region calls for a thorough analysis of today's and the anticipated future demand of young people for public services, especially in areas such as education, health and finance, and eventually a more innovative approach to the design and delivery of public policies and services. Indeed, good public governance will be essential to meet the needs of the youth population who will shape the future of the region over the coming decades.

Challenges impeding young people's transition to adulthood

Governance affects all aspects of young people's life. The methods and routines used in the formulation of legal texts, the working of public institutions and the implementation of policies impact the opportunities in the social, economic and political sphere. Governance frameworks can drive or impede the well-being of youth.

In the MENA region, governance challenges are placing heavy burdens on the development of young men and women. These deficiencies result in such diverse drawbacks as heavy administrative burdens discouraging youth entrepreneurs from launching a start-up or the lack of public spaces dedicated to youth, however, this report suggests that they share a common root cause: exclusive public governance arrangements. A more detailed diagnosis of how exclusive governance frameworks lock out young men and women from engagement in different spheres of public life will be discussed in greater detail in Chapter 3.

High levels of youth unemployment and economic inactivity

Unemployment among MENA youth hits young women with a punch as found nowhere else in the world. This finding points to governance failures and traditional social norms which impede their economic integration. While shortcomings in the governance frameworks of MENA countries are certainly not the only factor causing high levels of youth unemployment, they are rather neglected in the public discourse about how to create a healthy environment for job creation. Figure 2.2 shows that the MENA youth are facing the highest youth unemployment levels in the world with the younger generation in the Middle East facing an even tougher situation compared to their peers in North Africa.

Figure 2.2. **Youth unemployment rates by region, 2008-18**

15-24 year-olds

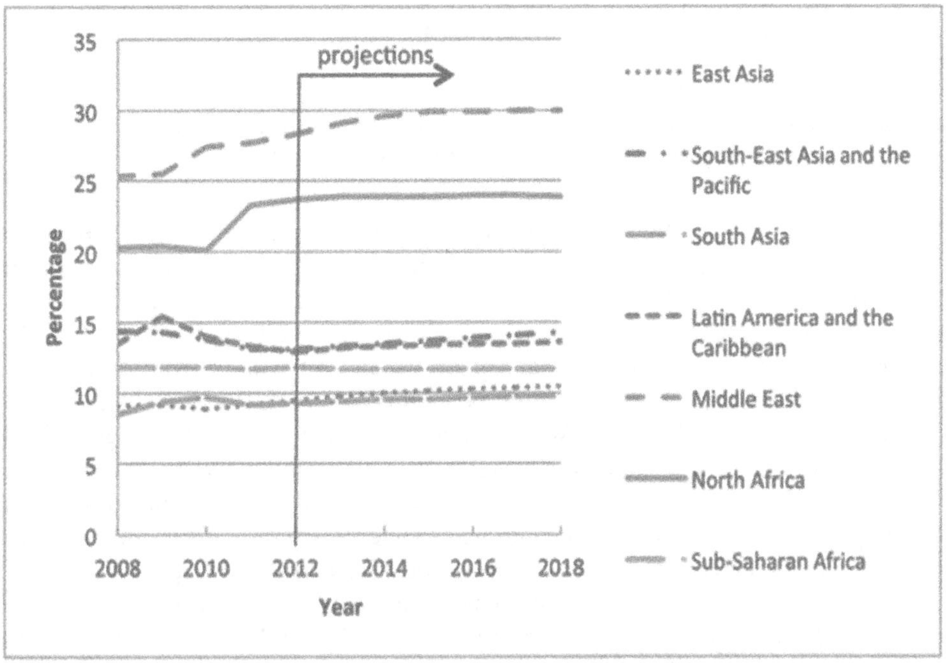

Source: Assaad, Ragui and Deborah Levison (2013), "Employment for youth – A growing challenge for the global economy," background research paper submitted to the High Level Panel on the Post-2015 Development Agenda, May www.post2015hlp.org/wp-content/uploads/2013/06/Assaad-Levison-Global-Youth-Employment-Challenge-Edited-June-5.pdf; ILO (2013), "Global employment trends: Recovering from a second jobs dip", ILO, Geneva, Switzerland, www.ilo.org/wcmsp5/groups/public/---dgreports/---dcomm/documents/publication/wcms_212423.pdf (accessed on 1 April 2016).

Figure 2.3 points to an upward trend in youth unemployment for most countries in recent years, in particular in Libya, Egypt and the Palestinian Authority. For Tunisia, the trend is more positive. After youth unemployment peaked at 43% in 2011, it decreased to 32% in 2014.

Figure 2.3. **Youth unemployment in selected MENA countries, 2014**

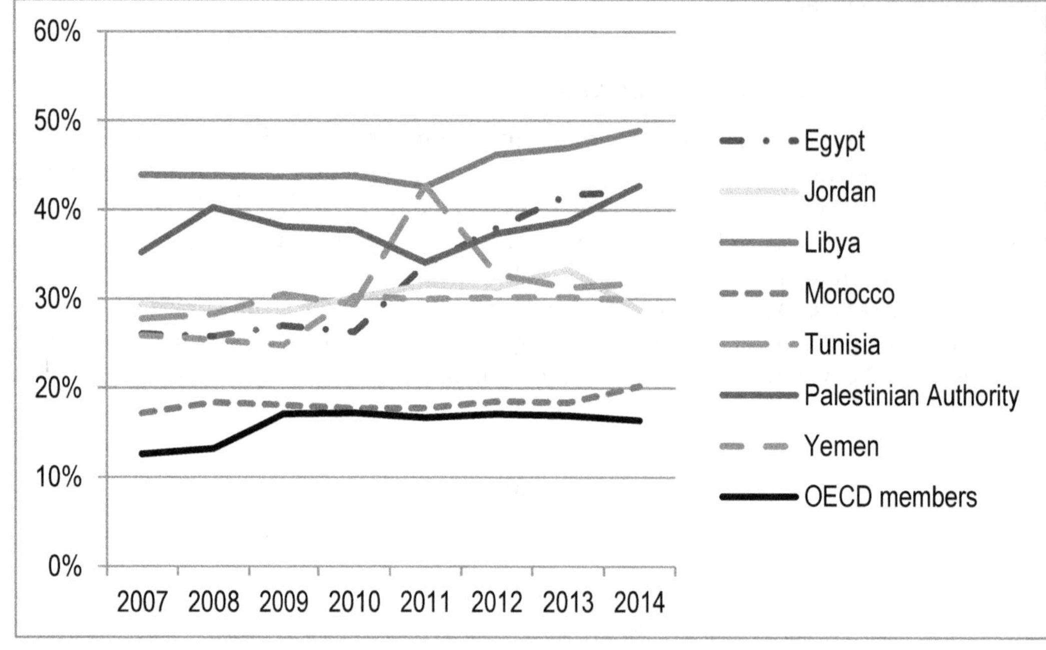

Source: OECD's own work based on World Bank (n.d.a), "Unemployment, youth total (percent of total labour force ages 15-24)", modeled ILO estimate (accessed on 10 April 2016).

While the youth unemployment rate is an important indicator to assess the economic activity of youth, it is not the most exact. Youth not in employment, education or training (NEET) offers better insights into how well countries manage the transition between school and work as it takes into account the proportion of youth studying (OECD, 2015). It captures the percentage of discouraged young men and women who either lack the motivation or the opportunity to find a job or improve their skills. However, NEET data for MENA countries is still scarce. While around 15% of young people (aged 15-29) in OECD countries are not in education, employment or training (NEET), the Moroccan Ministry of Youth and Sports estimates that more than half of all young Moroccans are neither employed nor in education or training. Available statistics from the International Labour Organization (ILO) for NEET youth (aged 15-24) in 2013 suggests that massive differences exist in the activity levels of young men and women. In Egypt, 17% of young men, but nearly 41% of young women are considered NEET while in the Palestinian Authority, around 25% of young men, but 38% of young females are considered economically inactive. Evidence from a survey conducted in Morocco suggests that the main reason for the staggering number of inactive young females in the country is opposition of their husband or parents (EuroMed, 2015). The structural and cultural barriers to equal opportunities for young women in the MENA region will be further discussed in Chapter 5.

Difficult transition from education into the job market

Formal education systems in MENA countries have been facing criticism for being unable to equip university graduates with the skills the private sector demands. In fact, well-educated graduates oftentimes face more difficulties in finding decent jobs than their peers without formal educational degrees. This finding highlights the mismatch between the supply and demand of skills as well as the fact that MENA countries have been unable to create jobs for a new generation of highly skilled young graduates who expect a fair return on their investment in long periods of education.

Figure 2.4 demonstrates that enrolment rates in all selected MENA countries are lagging behind those in OECD countries. Enrolment rates in secondary education vary between 83% and 91% in Tunisia, Jordan, Egypt and the Palestinian Authority, outnumbering Morocco (69%) and Yemen (47%). Despite significant progress in increasing the enrolment rates in Morocco over the last decade, 1.6 million young people in Morocco are still considered illiterate, of whom 70% live in rural areas, and the majority are women (EuroMed, 2015). With a view to enrolment in tertiary education, the figure shows similar results while the gap is considerably larger, both between MENA and OECD and among MENA countries. Recent years provide an uneven picture as enrolment rates for both secondary and tertiary education have fallen in some MENA countries while they have increased in others. These findings suggest that despite efforts to make education systems more inclusive, a significant share of young men and women still lacks access to basic education leaving them unprepared for participation in the labour market while highly skilled university graduates queue for economic opportunities.

Little weight in the political discourse and decision-making processes

In the selected MENA countries, the participation of young men and women in formal institutional political processes remains low. Indeed, their prominent role in the civil uprisings at the beginning of this decade did not result in greater involvement in forms of conventional participation, partly due to a lack of systematic efforts by governments to make them more accessible and appealing. Party affiliation is weak and low turnout levels for potential first-time voters reflect a disappointment with the existing structures and processes as they offer little prospect to drive change. Despite a pleasant engagement of MENA youth in civic activities and civil society organisations in some countries, youth representation in public consultations and fora with actual political weight tends to be marginal at best. The limited space for youth to raise their voice and shape political decisions is of even greater concern for vulnerable sub-groups such as young women or youth from rural areas and less fortunate socio-economic backgrounds. The marginalisation of youth and their concerns has resulted in youth attitudes towards political engagement that show little faith in politics and political institutions. This phenomenon will be discussed in greater detail in Chapter 3.

While some of the above presented phenomena are not unique to youth in the MENA region but challenge policy makers and youth alike around the globe, they weigh heavier in a context in which resources are scarce. In this context, an inadequate representation of youth needs may result in fewer public investments being channelled into critical pro-youth services.

Figure 2.4. **Enrolment in secondary and tertiary education in selected MENA countries, 2007-13**

A. Enrolment in secondary education

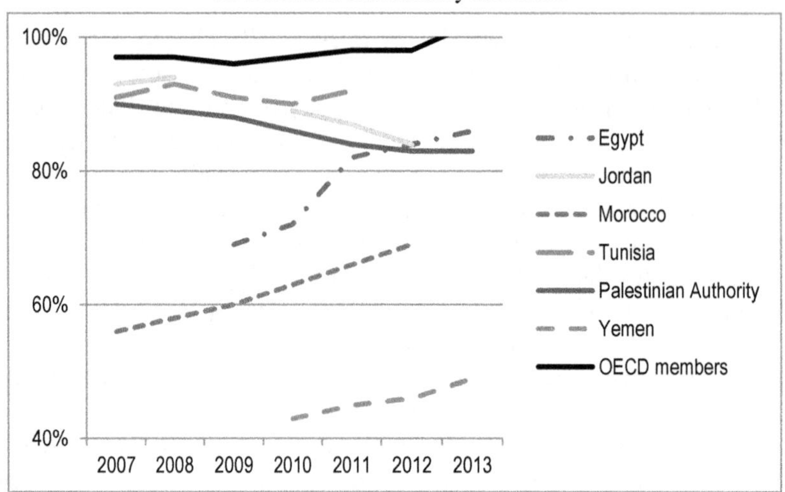

B. Enrolment in tertiary education

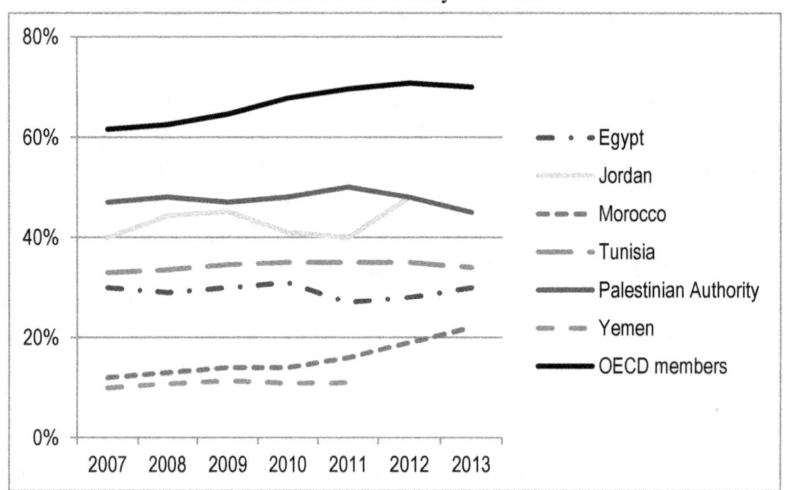

Source: World Bank (n.d. b), "School enrolment, secondary (% gross)", http://data.worldbank.org/indicator/SE.SEC.ENRR (accessed on 1 April 2016); World Bank (n.d. c), "School enrolment, tertiary (% gross)", http://data.worldbank.org/indicator/SE.TER.ENRR (accessed on 1 April 2016).

References

Assaad, Ragui and Deborah Levison (2013), "Employment for youth–A growing challenge for the global economy," background research paper submitted to the High Level Panel on the Post-2015 Development Agenda, May; www.post2015hlp.org/wp-content/uploads/2013/06/Assaad-Levison-Global-Youth-Employment-Challenge-Edited-June-5.pdf (accessed on 1 April 2016).

EuroMed (2015), *Le travail de jeunesse au Maroc et la participation des jeunes à l'échelon local*, May, www.euromedyouth.net/IMG/pdf/youth_work_morocco_fr_5_def.pdf (accessed on 1 April 2016).

ILO (2013), "Global Employment Trends: Recovering from a second jobs dip", ILO, Geneva, Switzerland, www.ilo.org/wcmsp5/groups/public/---dgreports/---dcomm/documents/publication/wcms_212423.pdf (accessed on 1 April 2016).

OECD (2015), *Investing in Youth: Tunisia: Strengthening the Employability of Youth during the Transition to a Green Economy*, OECD Publishing, Paris, http://dx.doi.org/10.1787/9789264226470-en.

United Nations (2013), *World Population Prospects: The 2012 Revision*, Department of Economic and Social Affairs, Population Division, DVD edition.

World Bank (n.d. a), "Unemployment, youth total (percent of total labour force ages 15-24)", modeled ILO estimate, http://data.worldbank.org/indicator/SL.UEM.1524.ZS (accessed on 10 April 2016).

World Bank (n.d. b), "School enrolment, secondary (% gross)", http://data.worldbank.org/indicator/SE.SEC.ENRR (accessed on 1 April 2016).

World Bank (n.d. c), "School enrolment, tertiary (% gross)", http://data.worldbank.org/indicator/SE.TER.ENRR (accessed on 1 April 2016).

Chapter 3

Towards a public governance framework for effective and inclusive youth engagement

As a cross-cutting policy area, youth policy in the MENA region suffers from the lack of a strategic and co-ordinated approach. In the absence of an integrated framework to define the "why", "how" and "what for" of youth policy, government interventions tend to be symbolic. As policy outcomes in favour of youth suffer from weak co-ordination and impact-orientation, MENA youth express significantly less trust in government than the age group of 50+. Against the two-fold challenge – young people's exclusion from the policy cycle and the lack of mainstreamed youth concerns in public policies and strategies – this chapter argues that governments should apply a "youth lens" to open government tools and traditional forms of policy making and integrate youth in governance processes that are typically left at the discretion of policy makers.

The different dimensions of engaging youth

When youth stand on the side while political decisions are being made, policy outcomes are unlikely to reflect their particular interests and needs. With the marginalisation of the younger generation in public institutions and processes, youth remain trapped in an observer status. Indeed, when MENA youth make it to the headlines, they do so as "bulge" or "challenge" and yet remain pushed into a passive role when political decisions are made.

Tackling the root cause of this phenomenon would require governments to encourage and develop more open and inclusive governance arrangements. OECD evidence shows that good public governance and inclusive institutions are relevant to achieve more inclusive growth patterns which benefit all parts of society (OECD, 2015a and 2015b). The findings suggest that governments pursuing greater transparency, access to information and stakeholder engagement will be successful in delivering more inclusive and better tailored policy outcomes. In turn, a government that is responsive to the needs of its citizens is likely to enjoy increasing levels of legitimacy and trust.

A view at the trust levels of MENA youth in their government reveals that, in all countries for which data is available, young people express significantly less trust than the age group of 50+ (Figure 3.1). Interestingly, this pattern contrasts with the average of OECD member countries in which youth expresses slightly more confidence in government than the older generation, although at a very low level.

Figure 3.1. **Gap in confidence in government by age group in selected MENA countries, 2015 (or latest available year)**

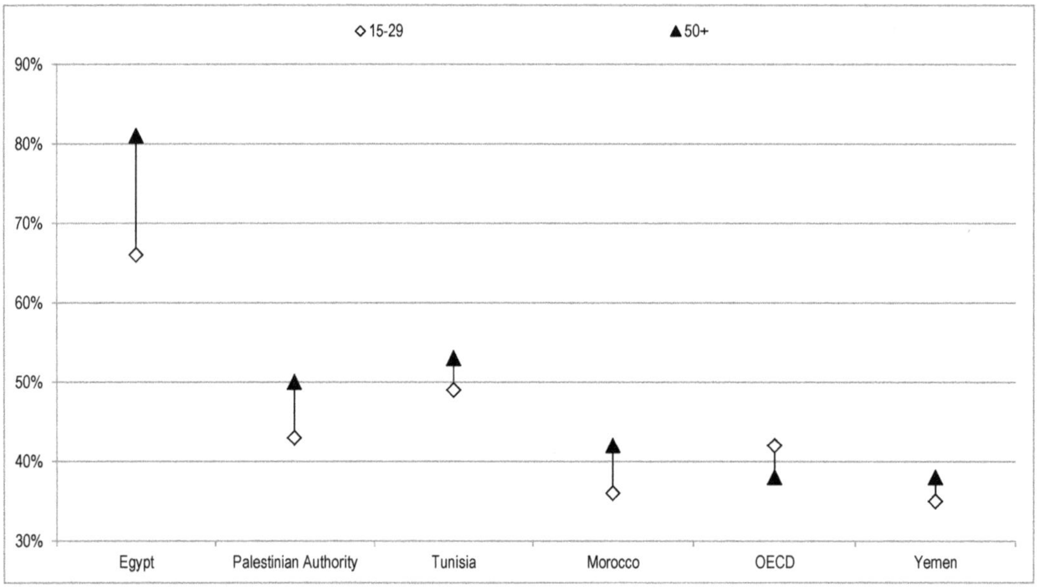

Note: Data for Egypt, OECD and Yemen relates to 2014; data for Morocco relates to 2013.
Source: OECD's own work based on data from the Gallup World Poll (2015).

Political engagement

Young people rightfully expect that governments will create conditions where all segments of society – poor and rich, male and female, urban and rural – can voice their ideas and demands. Youth associations, civil society and youth activists must be given real opportunities to engage in formal political processes with the power to shape policy outcomes and hold government officials accountable for their promises. Public consultation processes should be designed in such a way that they make it easy for young people to participate, including using both online and offline mechanisms. This is particularly critical given that the way political systems function in MENA countries and elsewhere frequently favours their marginalisation (e.g. voting age).

Social and economic empowerment

The need for a new public governance model is nowhere as obvious as in the failure of current arrangements to create economic opportunities for the young generation. The strategy of previous decades, which guaranteed government jobs to graduates, proved ruinous to the fiscal health of governments, economic growth and to the quality of government services. An alternative model in which the private sector would be the main job provider for skilled graduates does not seem to have emerged. The result has been a mismatch of youth needs and economic possibilities, leading to the withdrawal from economic activity of too many youth, particularly women, long periods spent searching for jobs, and the funnelling of many more youth into insecure, dead-end jobs in the informal sector. Queuing for jobs has important implications for social life, for instance when the lack of economic independence makes it impossible to leave the parental home and start a family.

Figure 3.2 proposes a set of ten questions to summarise what MENA youth should be able to expect from their governments. It points to the critical role public governance arrangements play for young people to engage, be empowered and benefit from policies and services that are tailored to their demands.

Figure 3.2. **Applying a youth lens to governance priorities: 10 key questions for policy makers**

1. Are government institutions sufficiently **open and transparent** to enable youth to hold government accountable?
2. Do youth enjoy opportunities to systematically **engage and participate** in decision making and public consultation processes?
3. Do governments make effective use of digital technologies and non-traditional channels to promote **youth engagement**?
4. Do legal frameworks and policies take into account the specific needs of young **women**, minority groups, and the disabled?
5. Are governance arrangements creating the conditions for **economic progress** that is both **inclusive and sustainable**?
6. Do governance frameworks translate economic progress into **economic opportunities** and **quality employment for youth**?
7. Are public services sufficiently **tailored, responsive and accountable** to the specific needs of young men and women?

8. Do **education, health and other public services** equip and support youth in making successful transitions to adulthood?
9. Are local governance frameworks allowing youth to participate in the identification of needs and promoting **communities** where youth can enjoy good quality of life?
10. Are solid frameworks for **integrity and the rule of law** in place to avoid misuse of public resources intended to serve youth purposes?

Source: OECD's own work.

A spotlight on public governance frameworks in MENA countries

The following sections provide a first analysis of the maturity of governance frameworks to bring youth in and mainstream their demands in the formulation and implementation of policies and services. By mainstreaming youth considerations, this report refers to the flexibility and capacity of any national social, economic and cultural policy framework to embed specific youth needs while pursuing general single- or multi-sector policy objectives, such as public health or job creation.

A whole-of-government approach to youth engagement and policy

As a cross-cutting policy area youth policy risks weak institutionalisation and co-ordination across departments and agencies. Youth programmes at sector level typically suffer from weak co-ordination between departments pursuing their own mandates and operating within their own organisational structures.

A whole-of-government (WoG) approach with strong leadership is vital to break up silo-based approaches and roll out youth policies and deliver youth services in a coherent manner across administrative boundaries. In line with the global trend, some of the selected MENA countries are currently formulating or implementing national youth policies with a view to incorporating sectoral strategies in favour of youth in a strategic policy document. Based on a vision for youth over a multi-year horizon, a national youth policy can improve coherence, stress areas where specific horizontal and vertical co-ordination mechanisms are required and assign clear mandates to key internal and external players that could be called upon to partner in setting and implementing the policy and its associated programming over time. By integrating youth in the formulation, implementation and monitoring of a holistic youth strategy, governments can ensure that related programmes and services are indeed responsive to their demands. Robust performance evaluation frameworks are required to assess whether the strategy delivers the intended results and, where adjustments are necessary, change course in order to achieve better results. However, the lack of youth-disaggregated data is a major obstacle to youth-sensitive programming. Without supportive data and information on the specific circumstances in which young men and women are living, public policies and services are likely to neglect their distinct demands as well as the heterogeneity of their interests.

The need for a co-ordinated approach to deliver youth policy is particularly evident in the transition of youth from education to employment. As youth move from school or university into the workforce, they rely on educational institutions to help them make career choices and gain the right skills. Therefore, the overall educational process should be linked with support from job placement programmes so that students gain access to internships, part-time work, or other skill-building opportunities. For example, industry development units and government placement programmes could interact with secondary or tertiary educational institutions to help shape curricula and provide information to students. Workforce development boards, such as the examples referred to in the *OECD Territorial Review of the Chicago Tri-State Metropolitan Area* (OECD, 2012) can place around a single table businesses, labour unions, governments and training service providers (e.g. schools and private sector firms) to link jobs to skills, tailor training curricula to meet actual job requirements and generate apprenticeship possibilities for first-time jobs.

Reality on the ground in MENA countries shows a different picture. Previous efforts have been characterised by significant challenges to move from formulation to effective implementation due to unclear responsibilities, limited capacities for co-ordination and the absence of effective accountability mechanisms. Formal responsibility for youth policy and programme co-ordination typically lies with the Ministry of Youth, a ministry with often combined portfolios such as youth and sports, and so far fairly limited capacities to steer and co-ordinate a national vision for youth across administrative boundaries. The lack of adequate capacities raises serious barriers to programme effectiveness. Limited resource control and oversight responsibility have impeded mainstreaming youth concerns across the policy spectrum and translating plans into action.

The legal foundations for youth engagement and policy

Whereas youth-related provisions in the Constitution only provide a first indication of a country's commitment to promote youth engagement and policy, the different extent to which MENA countries refer to youth is striking.

Table 3.1 shows that the most recently drafted constitutions in Egypt (2014), Tunisia (2014) and Morocco (2011) are the most progressive in terms of assigning rights and freedoms to youth. Young people have been strong advocates for constitutional change and the positive outcomes on paper can be attributed to their unprecedented visibility in the public debate. In Morocco, with the pending creation of the Advisory Council of Youth and Associations (*Conseil Consultatif de la Jeunesse et de l'Action Associative*), the participation of youth is expected to become institutionalised in formal terms. Moreover, the Constitution requests local authorities to take into account the concerns of young people whose active participation shall be facilitated through associations and municipal youth councils (see Chapter 4). In the wake of the popular movements in Tunisia, the adoption of the decree 2011-88 on the formation and funding of associations has resulted in a mushrooming of youth-led civil society organisations and youth associations (EuroMed, 2013).

The provisions addressing youth endorse their active role in various areas of life stressing the need to create an environment in which they can fulfil their potential and assume responsibilities. Youth are pictured as a source of creativity, innovation and energy. The most recent adjustments highlight an increasing understanding of the need to institutionalise young people's representation – either by assigning a minimum share of seats in local councils in Egypt, the creation of a consultative council for youth in Morocco or a more vague reference to an appropriate representation of youth in local councils in Tunisia and the first House of Representatives in Egypt. The Libyan interim Constitution of 2011 and the 2003 Basic Law in the Palestinian Authority discuss the obligation of the government to take care of adolescents in the context of supporting the family as the basis of society.

Table 3.1. **References to youth in the constitutions of selected MENA countries, 2014 (or latest available year)**

Egypt (2014)	*Article 82* The state guarantees the care of youth and young children, in addition to helping them discover their talents and developing their cultural, scientific, psychological, creative and physical abilities, encouraging them to engage in group and volunteer activity and enabling them to take part in public life. *Article 180: Election of local councils* The law regulates other conditions for candidacy and procedures of election, provided that one quarter of the seats are allocated to youth under 35 years old. *Article 244: Representation for youth, Christians, disabled persons, etc.* The state grants youth, Christians, persons with disability and expatriate Egyptians appropriate representation in the first House of Representatives to be elected after this Constitution is adopted, in the manner specified by law. *Source:* www.constituteproject.org/constitution/Egypt_2014.pdf.
Jordan 1952 (amended in1984)	-
Libya (2011)* * Libyan interim Constitutional Declaration	*Article 5* Family shall be the basis of society and shall be protected by the State. The State shall protect and encourage marriage. The State shall guarantee the protection of motherhood, childhood and old age and look after children, young people and persons with special needs. *Source*: www.constituteproject.org/constitution/Libya_2011.pdf.
Morocco (2011)	*Article 33* It is incumbent on the public powers to take all the appropriate measures with a view to: • stimulate and make general the participation of youth in the social, economic, cultural and political life of the country; • aid the young to establish themselves in [an] active and associative life and to give assistance to them in the difficulty of scholarly, social or professional adaptation; • facilitate the access of the young to culture, to science, to technology, to art, to sports and to leisure, all in creation of propitious conditions for the full deployment of their creative and innovative potential in all these domains. A Consultative Council of Youth and of Associative Action [Conseil consultative de la jeunesse et de l'action associative], is created. *Article 170* The Consultative Council of Youth and of Associative Action [Conseil consultatif de la jeunesse et de l'action associative], created by virtue of Article 33 of this Constitution, is a consultative instance within the domains of the protection of youth and of the promotion of associative life. It is charged to study and to follow the questions [of] interest to these domains and to formulate the proposals on any subject of economic, social and cultural order [of] direct interest to youth and associative action, as well as the development of the creative energies of youth, and their inducement [incitation] to participation in the national life, in the spirit of responsible citizenship. *Source*: www.constitutionnet.org/files/morocco_eng.pdf .
Tunisia (2014)	*Article 8* Youth are an active force in building the nation. The state seeks to provide the necessary conditions for developing the capacities of youth and realising their potential, supports them to assume responsibility, and strives to extend and generalise their participation in social, economic, cultural and political development.. *Article 133* The elections law shall guarantee the representation of youth in local authority councils. *Source*: www.constituteproject.org/constitution/Tunisia_2014.pdf.
Palestinian Authority (2003)* *Basic law is to function as a temporary constitution	*Article 48* The state shall guarantee care for families, motherhood, and childhood. It shall care for adolescents and the youth. The law shall regulate the rights of the child, mother and family in accordance with the provisions of international agreements and the "Charter of the Rights of the Arab Child." In particular, the state shall seek to provide protection for children from harm, harsh treatment, exploitation, and from any work that would endanger their safety, health and education. *Source*: www.palestinianbasiclaw.org/basic-law/2003-permanent-constitution-draft.

Countries may not refer to youth in their Constitution, but encourage their empowerment through a set of policies or a distinct national youth policy. In OECD countries, references to youth in the Constitution are few and completely absent in countries like Australia, Canada and France. In Germany, the Basic Law refers to the protection of young persons to justify the limits and possible restriction of basic principles such as the freedom of expression and movement (Deutscher Bundestag, 2012). Positive rights granted by the Constitution exist in Italy (Art. 31: protection of mothers, children and the young by adopting necessary provisions)[1] and Spain (Section 48: The public authorities shall promote conditions for the free and effective participation of young people in political, social, economic and cultural development).[2]

The formulation and implementation of a national youth policy

Youth as a public policy field cuts across many different policy areas including employment, education, health, justice and sports. National youth policies have emerged as a guiding framework to shape a vision for youth and to mobilise and co-ordinate political support beyond one-time events by stressing synergies between youth policies and other strategic policy documents. In the United Kingdom, for instance, the 2010 national youth strategy, "Positive for Youth" develops a vision for a youth-friendly society along three key parameters (i.e. supportive relationships, strong ambitions, good opportunities). Designed for youth aged 13 to 19, the strategy sets out a series of policies and government initiatives with the objective of unlocking social mobility, tackling child poverty, preventing youth crime, and reducing health inequalities. The strategy puts a strong emphasis on local partnerships between communities, charities, local businesses and local councils to apply youth policy in a place-based fashion. It features a plan to monitor and evaluate programme implementation (UK Government, 2011).

Box 3.1 presents the Irish cross-Government "National Strategy on Children and Young People's Participation in Decision-making 2015-2020". Ireland was the first country in Europe to develop a strategy across the government dedicated to strengthening the voice of children and young people in political decision making.

Box 3.1. **The Irish cross-Government National Strategy on Children and Young People's Participation in Decision-making (2015-2020)**

In the formulation process of the strategy, youth stakeholders were invited to participate in the identification of objectives and activities including:

- a national consultation with 66 700 children and young people
- a public consultation with over 1 000 stakeholders
- bilateral consultative meetings with relevant government departments and state agencies
- bilateral consultative meetings with relevant independent statutory agencies, such as the Ombudsman for Children and the Mental Health Commission
- bilateral consultative meetings with children's and youth non-government organisations
- a literature review to assess progress to date and identify gaps and areas for development
- an audit of existing nationwide activity enabling children and young people's participation in decision making

Box 3.1. **The Irish cross-Government National Strategy on Children and Young People's Participation in Decision-making (2015-2020)** *(continued)*

- a review of monitoring and evaluation reports of children's participation initiatives in the previous ten years
- commissioned targeted research on children's participation in decision making.

The strategy, launched in June 2015, presents the following objectives and priority areas for action:

1. Children and young people will have a voice in decisions made in their local communities.
2. Children and young people will have a voice in decision making in early education, schools and the wider formal and non-formal education systems.
3. Children and young people will have a voice in decisions that affect their health and well-being, including on the health and social services delivered to them.
4. Children and young people will have a voice in the Courts and legal system.

The strategy contains a series of additional objectives, which include:

5. Promoting effective leadership to champion and promote participation of children and young people.
6. Development of education and training for professionals working with and on behalf of children and young people.
7. Mainstreaming the participation of children and young people in the development of policy, legislation and research.

The priority action in the strategy for the Department of Children and Youth Affairs (DCYA) is the establishment of a Children and Young People's Participation Hub, as a national centre for excellence. The Hub will support Government departments and other organisations in implementing the strategy through training, documenting best practice and working with education institutions to oversee the development of education on children's rights for professionals who work with and for children and young people. The Hub will also host a comprehensive online database of practical resources and literature.

The DCYA has a dedicated Citizen Participation Unit, the role of which is to ensure that children and young people have a voice in the design, delivery and monitoring of services and policies that affect their lives, at national and local level. It collaborates in this endeavour with other government departments, statutory bodies and non-government organisations.

Source: Department of Children and Youth Affairs (2015), "National Strategy on Children and Young People's Participation in Decision-making, 2015–2020", Government Publications, Dublin, http://dcya.gov.ie/documents/playandrec/20150617NatStratParticipationReport.pdf (accessed on 23 March 2016).

Although no single, unified framework exists to guide policy makers in setting, implementing and monitoring youth policy, Bacalso and Farrow (2016) notice "a growing international consensus on principles for youth policy making". Building on international frameworks such as the 1998 Lisbon Declaration on Youth Policies and Programmes and the 2007 World Programme of Action for Youth (WPAY) as well as individual contributions to the debate, such as by Peter Lauritzen (1993),[3] their paper extracts a set of eight principles to guide the development and performance evaluation of youth policies. They are summarised in Box 3.2. The principles identified by the two authors are similar to the eight principles identified by the Baku Commitment to Youth Policies (2014), which were identified by over 700 participants from 165 countries in the First Global Forum on Youth Policies on 28-30 October 2014 in the capital city of Azerbaijan.

Box 3.2. **Towards a set of guiding principles for (national) youth policy**

1. Democratic and participatory: Legitimised through a democratically elected Parliament; inclusion and full participation of actors such as youth professionals, civil society, youth organisations and movements as well as young people; participation in the design and implementation; genuine sharing of power between decision makers and young people; inclusive delivery from state, private and non-profit sectors.

2. Cross-sectoral and transversal: Holistic approach cutting across all policy domains, and going beyond typical "youth" issues; recognition of the diversity of backgrounds, experiences, needs and aspirations within the "youth" demographic; participation and empowerment of vulnerable youth.

3. Coherent and co-ordinated: Consider viability in the current political context; clear framework, based on rights, needs and well-being to ensure consistency; inclusive, multi-level and multi-stakeholder co-ordination of policy.

4. Researched and evidence-based: Ongoing, consistent, independent youth research; long-term documenting of developments and changes, skilled researchers and a body of national knowledge on youth sociology; evidence-based policy making; inclusion of objective and subjective measures.

5. Fairly budgeted and fairly financed: Allocated resources linked to objectives of youth policy and the demands of young people; independence of youth and youth focused organisations; remuneration of youth sector professionals.

6. Competent and professional: Recognition of youth work as a profession; quality standards for youth work and youth sector professionals at national level.

7. Monitored and evaluated: Effective monitoring mechanisms to evaluate policy performance and strengthen accountability; incorporation of youth-led research; organisational and institutional feedback and learning processes; national and local indicators to measure the success of policies; inclusion of external, independent evaluators; effective follow-up based on performance outcomes.

8. Open and freely accessible: Announcement of decision-making processes (renewal of policies); participation of young people, experts and stakeholders with opportunities to influence decisions and processes fairly; transparency through publication of information on decisions, budgets, beneficiaries and evaluations.

Source: Bacalso, Cristina and Alex Farrow (2016), "Youth policies from around the world: International practices and country examples", *Youth Policy Working Paper*, No 1, March 2016, www.youthpolicy.org/library/wp-content/uploads/library/Youth_Policy_Working_Paper_01_201603.pdf (accessed on 10 April 2016).

At regional level, the African Youth Charter, issued by the African Union in 2006, provides guidance for the elaboration of a holistic national youth policy. As of 2016, 36 member states have ratified the Charter including Tunisia (2011) and Libya (2008). Egypt has signed the Charter but has not ratified it. Beyond the principles outlined above, the Charter stresses that the national youth policy should be framed within a country's national development framework. It highlights the institutional aspects of young people's representation in decision-making processes and suggests the appointment of youth focal points in government structures, as well as the establishment of national youth co-ordinating mechanisms. Most notably, the Charter calls for effective and inclusive co-ordination mechanisms for young men and women to engage across the policy cycle.

Table 3.2 offers a summary of the status and main features of youth strategies in the selected MENA countries. As of April 2016, Morocco and Jordan have formulated a national youth policy. In Tunisia, the government announced its intention to organise a series of consultations with youth at regional and local levels to prepare an integrated national youth strategy covering a multi-year horizon. National youth strategies have been formulated in Jordan and the Palestinian Authority in previous years, however, moving from planning to implementation has turned out to be a major challenge. In fact, many initiatives have been donor-driven with limited follow-up and accountability mechanisms in place. In Yemen, the serious deterioration of the security situation has resulted in a virtual standstill of the implementation of the youth policy for 2006-15.

The institutional representation of youth

The governments of the countries covered in this report have taken parallel approaches to organise the co-ordination of youth policies across government departments and agencies. Table 3.3 summarises the available information on bodies with responsibility for youth affairs. The principle option chosen is a dedicated ministry – regularly including sports as a second portfolio. The representation of youth issues through youth federations does not have a strong tradition as the largely donor-driven creation of these councils has not turned out to be sustainable.

Table 3.2. **Does a national youth policy exist in the selected MENA countries?**

Country	Status and main features of youth policy articulation
Egypt	The 2010 Human Development Report for Egypt, focusing on youth, outlined a National Policy for Youth developed in 2009 by the National Youth Council, but this organisation has now been disbanded.
Jordan	National youth strategies were developed in co-operation with the United Nations Development Programme (UNDP) for the 2005-09 period and a national employment plan giving priority to youth employment was developed with support from the International Labour Organization (ILO) for 2011-20. The former identifies nine priorities: youth participation, civil rights and citizenship, recreational activities and leisure time, culture and information, information technology and globalisation, education and training, employment, health, and environment. Reportedly, the National Youth Strategy was reviewed and launched anew in 2010 for the period of 2011-15. A National Youth Strategy for 2016-18 has been developed.
Libya	Libya ratified the African Union Youth Charter in 2008. The current situation in Libya has prevented advance in plans to develop a youth policy to build on the constitutional declaration's call for the state to play a lead role in taking care of children, youth and the handicapped.
Morocco	The Integrated National Youth Strategy (*Stratégie Nationale Intégrée de la Jeunesse*, SNIJ) 2015-30 was published in 2014 by the Ministry of Youth and Sport and the General Direction of Local Communities with support from international organisations. The strategy "is part of a general ambition to place young people at the heart of public policies" and to address the relevant provisions in the new 2011 Constitution. It claims to provide an integrated strategic vision for youth-related planning and programming and to integrate the different sectoral actions in place. It identifies five fields of intervention: *1)* increasing economic opportunities for young people and promote their employability; *2)* increasing access and quality of basic services for youth and reduce geographic disparities; *3)* promoting the active participation of youth in social and civic life and in decision making; *4)* promoting respect for human rights; *5)* strengthening the institutional arrangements for communication, information, evaluation and governance. The implementation of the strategy will be facilitated by an Action Plan (2015--30) outlining priority measures, performance indicators, responsibilities and a budget framework.
Palestinian Authority	Although a National Youth Policy Planning Document was prepared in 2005 and a Youth Cross-cutting Strategy was drafted in 2011, both of these processes are currently on hold. The latter plan sets out four strategic objectives: participation, citizenship and rights, empowerment, and access.
Tunisia	Tunisia ratified the African Youth Charter in 2011. Tunisia is currently organising a consultation process with youth to inform the formulation of an Integrated National Youth Strategy.
Yemen	Yemen issued a youth policy covering the 2006-15 period specifying interventions for children and youth. Interventions for Yemenis in the 15-24 age group included: *1)* creating a National Youth Employment Environment and Plan; *2)* strengthening national identify, youth inclusion, and participation; *3)* increasing leisure options and creating child/youth friendly urban planning; and *4)* preventing early pregnancy and reducing the risks to reproductive health.

Source: Youthpolicy.org (n.d.), "Factsheets", www.youthpolicy.org/factsheets (accessed on 12 April 2016); Ministry of Youth and Sports in Morocco (2014), *Stratégie Nationale Intégrée de la Jeunesse 2015-30*, www.mjs.gov.ma/sites/default/files/strategie-morocco.pdf; EuroMed (2014), *Le travail de jeunesse et l'employabilité des jeunes en Jordanie*, June, http://euromedyouth.net/IMG/pdf/def_on_line_jorda_de_roule__jordanie__fr.pdf (accessed on 1 April 2016).

Table 3.3. **Bodies with formal responsibility for youth affairs in selected MENA countries, 2016**

Country	Ministry	National youth council	Youth federation
Egypt	**Ministry of Youth and Sports**	*(Disbanded)*	*(Revolutionary Youth Council disbanded)*
Jordan	**Ministry of Youth**		Jordan Youth Innovation Forum (40 organisations)
Libya	**Ministry of Youth and Sports**		Libyan Youth Forum
Morocco	**Ministry of Youth and Sports**	*(National youth council included in 2011 Constitution, but not yet operational)*	
Palestinian Authority		**Higher Council for Youth and Sports**	*Palestinian Youth Legislative Council (donor initiative; apparently under reorganisation)*
Tunisia	**Ministry of Youth and Sports**		*Tunisian Union of Youth Organizations (UTOJ; disbanded)*
Yemen	**Ministry of Youth and Sports**		National Youth Council Committee representing local youth councils (donor initiative)

Note: The principal entity responsible for youth policy and programme co-ordination in each country is shown in **bold**. Disbanded entities and those mandated, but not yet operational, are shown in *italics*.

Source: Youthpolicy.org (n.d.), "Factsheets", www.youthpolicy.org/factsheets (accessed on 12 April 2016) and organisational websites.

In several countries, the youth portfolio is assigned to a Ministry of Youth and Sport although the youth portfolio itself is generally not well-funded. Cross-cutting youth councils, which existed in some MENA countries in the past with the objective to facilitate co-ordination across youth-oriented organisations, generally did not have a mandate permitting them to direct the activities of line ministries, nor did they benefit from a powerful link to the Centre of Government, such as the office of the Prime Minister or President. In light of these experiences, the case for a clearly mandated responsibility centre for youth policy is obvious. The lead institutions should be assigned adequate capacities and competencies to fulfil their role in co-ordinating the identification of youth needs and delivery of services, both vertically and horizontally across the government. The cross-cutting nature of youth policy requires a clear definition of the mandates for each entity involved, with these mandates communicated broadly across the administrative system and the public, and effective co-ordination mechanisms to avoid fragmented coverage. An institutionalised link to a higher office in the Centre of Government can facilitate the exercise of control over the range of activities necessary to integrate youth-related programming. For instance, since 2015, with the appointment of the Prime Minister as the Minister of Intergovernmental Affairs and Youth in Canada, youth is a part of the Prime Minister's portfolio. In the absence of a performant lead institution, when demands for reform to address unmet youth needs arise, they are too often met by making marginal changes, such as reassigning smaller units from one ministry to another.

Effective vertical co-ordination is critical to ensure that the national vision for youth indeed translates into better access to quality employment, education, health and other services on the ground. In turn, strong links between the different levels of government are critical to ensure that local public authorities and non-government stakeholders, starting with youth groups themselves, are fully integrated into the process of policy design, delivery and evaluation.

The OECD Recommendation of the Council on Gender Equality in Public Life provides useful guidance for strengthening the institutional framework to mainstream a cross-cutting policy field (see Box 3.3).

Box 3.3. **The Recommendation of the Council on Gender Equality in Public Life: The institutional framework to mainstream gender equality**

Establish an institutional framework to ensure the effective implementation, co-ordination and sustainability of the gender equality and mainstreaming strategy, by:

1. Establishing clear roles, responsibilities, mandates and lines of accountability of key governmental and oversight bodies in implementing gender equality and mainstreaming initiatives.
2. Bolstering the capacities and resources of gender equality institutions to facilitate a consistent response at appropriate levels of government and to develop, implement and monitor gender-sensitive programmes and policies throughout the government, based on gender-disaggregated statistics and indicators. Effectiveness of gender equality institutions can also be strengthened by placing them at the highest possible level in the government.
3. Ensuring the capacity and resources of public institutions to integrate gender equality perspectives in their activities, for example, by identifying gender equality focal points across governmental bodies, by investing resources in training and promoting collaborative approaches with knowledge centres to produce gender-sensitive knowledge, leadership and communication, by ensuring the collection of gender and gender-disaggregated statistics in their areas of responsibility and by providing clear guidelines, tools, communication and expectations to public institutions in this area.
4. Strengthening vertical and horizontal co-ordination mechanisms for policy coherence across governmental bodies and levels of government that involve relevant non-governmental stakeholders to ensure synergies and effective implementation of gender equality initiatives.

Source: OECD (2016), *2015 OECD Recommendation of the Council on Gender Equality in Public Life*, OECD Publishing, Paris, http://dx.doi.org/10.1787/9789264252820-en.

In some MENA countries, youth houses or centres (*maisons de jeunes*) provide yet another institutional framework for the government to reach out to young people. In Morocco, a network of around 500 youth houses exists to support the capacities of registered youth organisations and encourage the social inclusion and participation of young people in local sport, cultural and leisure activities. With an annual budget of less than EUR 300, the youth houses suffer from inadequate capacities to provide the kind of services and activities that young people hope to have access to. Moreover, the existing youth houses are distributed unequally across the territory. Youth houses in Tunisia, which provide non-formal education opportunities and serve as community centres for non-governmental associations engaged in youth work, face similar challenges (EuroMed, 2013). A network of youth centres also exists in Jordan.

Applying a "youth lens" to public governance arrangements

This section sets out the analytical framework of this report. It suggests that public governance, the system of strategic processes and tools, as well as institutions, rules and interactions for effective policy making, can impede or further inclusive and effective youth engagement and policy.

Two challenges of the youth-public governance relationship in MENA countries stand out. First, the exclusion of young men and women from the political arena and decision-making processes is leaving them at the margin of the public debate with little scope to shape policy outcomes in their favour. Their marginalisation in public life risks reproducing a vicious cycle of frustration with the performance of government officials, decreasing levels of youth trust in government, and a gradual disengagement from politics. This is a challenge the selected MENA countries share with many OECD member countries. Exclusive governance arrangements tend to favour narrow elites at the expense of transparency and accountability as well as a fair distribution of social and economic benefit among the generations. Second, in the absence of youth at the decision-making table, they deplore a weak integration of their concerns in strategic policy documents and the delivery of public services.

This report is the first of its kind to apply a "youth lens" to public governance arrangements. Against the background of this two-fold challenge – the exclusion of young people from the policy cycle and the lack of mainstreamed youth concerns in public policies and strategies – it argues that existing public governance arrangements need to be readjusted towards the demands of the younger generation.

The analytical framework builds on the OECD approach to open government which argues that more open, transparent, inclusive and accountable government can boost more inclusive policy outcomes and inclusive growth (see Figure 3.3).

Figure 3.3. **The OECD open government theory of change**

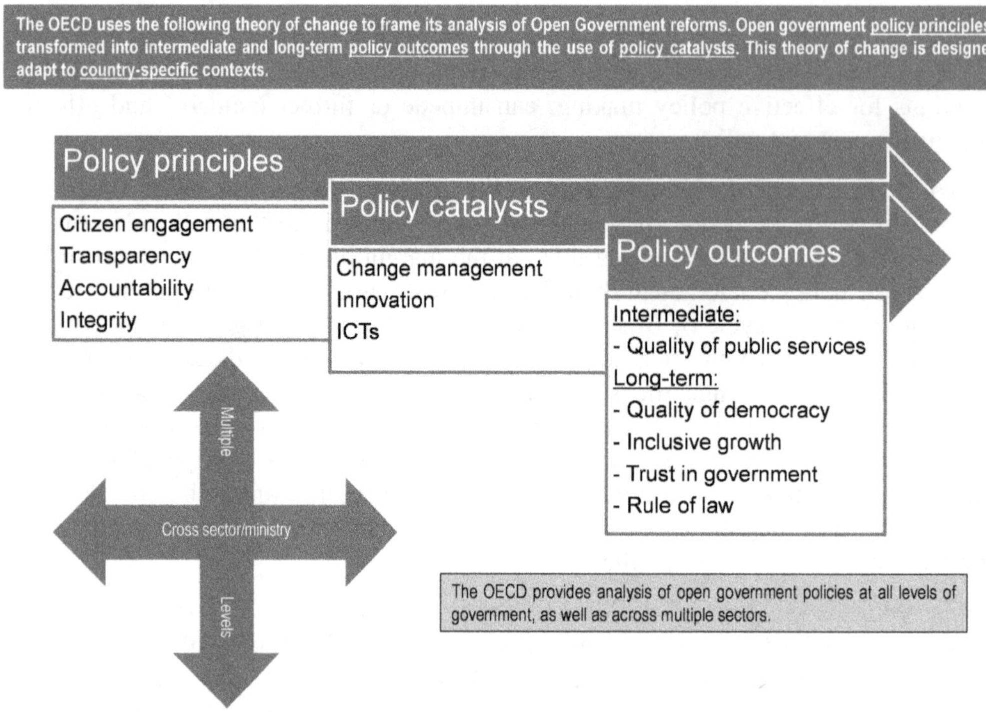

The OECD uses the following theory of change to frame its analysis of Open Government reforms. Open government policy principles are transformed into intermediate and long-term policy outcomes through the use of policy catalysts. This theory of change is designed to adapt to country-specific contexts.

Policy principles
Citizen engagement
Transparency
Accountability
Integrity

Policy catalysts
Change management
Innovation
ICTs

Policy outcomes
Intermediate:
- Quality of public services
Long-term:
- Quality of democracy
- Inclusive growth
- Trust in government
- Rule of law

Multiple
Cross sector/ministry
Levels

The OECD provides analysis of open government policies at all levels of government, as well as across multiple sectors.

Source: OECD (2015c), "The OECD - A partner in open government", www.oecd.org/mena/governance/open-government.htm; www.slideshare.net/OECD-GOV/open-government-brochure.

Open government redefines the way in which government processes, policies and data should be produced, used and made available to the public. Opening up information and decision-making processes to a broader audience will lead to better informed policies and services. Institutional reforms to achieve greater transparency and public participation have a crucial role to play in increasing public scrutiny and oversight and fighting corruption. MENA countries have started to commit themselves to promoting more open and inclusive policy making and institutions. Through the Open Government Partnership (OGP), and with the assistance of the OECD, Tunisia, Morocco, Jordan, Libya, the Palestinian Authority and Lebanon have begun to engage in a dialogue with civil society. Tunisia and Jordan have consulted with civil society in drafting and implementing their OGP Action Plans.

The ongoing reform processes offer an opportune moment for governments to apply a "youth lens" to open government tools (e.g. access to information frameworks; citizen engagement; digital technologies) and traditional forms of policy making. By applying a youth lens to access to information frameworks, for instance, this report refers to concrete measures that would tailor government information to youth needs and bring youth into the process of collecting, sharing and scrutinising youth-disaggregated data. Applying a youth lens to open government tools redirects the focus from a rather abstract notion of "citizens" to an immediate beneficiary (and potential contributor to the elaboration and implementation) of public policies and services.

Moreover, a shared understanding would be necessary that public governance frameworks set the framework in which youth seek opportunities in economic, social and public life. So far, the restrictions for young people to engage set by existing institutions, rules and interactions for policy making are not yet discussed in the public debate to the extent that was necessary.

By integrating youth in governance processes that are typically left at the discretion of policy makers, such as the allocation of public budgets, governments can work towards mainstreaming youth considerations across the whole of government. A youth-sensitive approach to the allocation of public expenditures, for instance, could provide a space for youth to identify their needs, co-design programmes and co-decide on spending priorities. Their engagement across the policy cycle, before the allocation of public funds to specific programmes, is just one example of various areas in which young men and women can play a much more active and constructive role than is currently the case.

Figure 3.4 introduces the analytical framework for applying a youth lens to public governance.

Figure 3.4. **The analytical framework: Applying a youth lens to public governance**

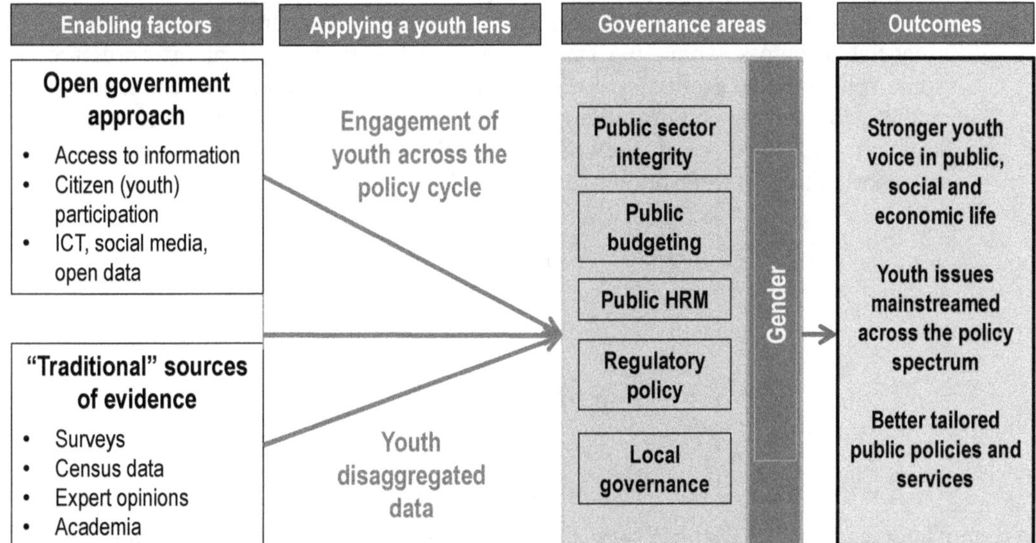

Source: OECD's own work.

The analytical framework is discussed in greater detail in the following two chapters. Chapter 4 highlights the positive outcomes of applying a "youth lens" to open government tools and traditional forms of policy making before Chapter 5 outlines some of the public governance processes and areas (e.g. public sector integrity, regulatory policy, public budgeting, public human resource management, local governance and gender) in which young men and women can play a more active role to ensure their considerations are mainstreamed in the formulation and delivery of public policies and services.

As the youth-governance connection has received limited attention heretofore, this discussion will be exploratory.

Notes

1. *Senato della Repubblica* (Constitution of the Italian Republic), adopted in 1947, www.senato.it/documenti/repository/istituzione/costituzione_inglese.pdf (accessed on 1 April 2016).
2. *Congreso de los Diputados* (Spanish Constitution), adopted in 1978, www.congreso.es/portal/page/portal/Congreso/Congreso/Hist_Normas/Norm/const_espa_texto_ingles_0.pdf (accessed on 1 April 2016).
3. In 1992, Lauritzen (1993) identified eight indicators, which together make up a national or international youth policy: 1) legislation concerning young people; 2) financial resources within the state budget; 3) non-governmental infrastructure; 4) some voluntary and professional training structure; 5) independent research into youth matters; 6) advisory bodies to the government; 7) communication network at national, regional and local level between authorities, youth movements and agencies; 8) opportunities for innovation and development.

References

African Union (2006), African Youth Charter, www.au.int/en/sites/default/files/treaties/7789-file-african_youth_charter.pdf (accessed on 1 April 2016).

Bacalso, Cristina and Alex Farrow (2016), "Youth policies from around the world: International practices and country examples", *Youth Policy Working Paper*, No. 1, March 2016, www.youthpolicy.org/library/wp-content/uploads/library/Youth_Policy_Working_Paper_01_201603.pdf (accessed on 10 April 2016).

Congreso de los Diputados (1978), "Constitution", www.congreso.es/portal/page/portal/Congreso/Congreso/Hist_Normas/Norm/const_espa_texto_ingles_0.pdf (accessed on 1 April 2016).

Deutscher Bundestag (2012), "Basic Law for the Federal Republic of Germany", November, www.bundestag.de/blob/284870/ce0d03414872b427e57fccb703634dcd/basic_law-data.pdf (accessed on 1 April 2016).

Department of Children and Youth Affairs (2015), "National Strategy on Children and Young People's Participation in Decision-making, 2015–2020", Government

Publications, Dublin, http://dcya.gov.ie/documents/playandrec/20150617NatStratParticipationReport.pdf (accessed on 23 March 2016).

EuroMed (2014), *Le travail de jeunesse et l'employabilité des jeunes en Jordanie*, June, http://euromedyouth.net/IMG/pdf/def_on_line_jorda_de_roule__jordanie__fr.pdf (accessed on 1 April 2016).

EuroMed (2013), *Le travail de jeunesse en Tunisie après la révolution*, September, http://euromedyouth.net/IMG/pdf/tunisie_apre_s_re_volution_fr.pdf_02-09-13_def.pdf (accessed on 1 April 2016).

Gallup World Poll (2015). http://www.gallup.com/services/170945/world-poll.aspx (accessed on 10 April 2016).

International IDEA (trans.) (2014), "Egypt's Constitution of 2014", Constitute., www.constituteproject.org/constitution/Egypt_2014.pdf (accessed on 1 April 2016).

Lauritzen, P. (1993), "Youth policy structures in Europe, including 8 indicators for a national youth policy", in Ohana, Y. and A. Rothemund (2008), *Eggs in a Pan*, www.coe.int/t/dg4/youth/Source/Resources/Publications/Peter_Lauritzen_book_en.pdf (accessed on 10 April 2016).

Ministry of Youth and Sports in Morocco (2014), *Stratégie Nationale Intégrée de la Jeunesse 2015-30*, www.mjs.gov.ma/sites/default/files/strategie-morocco.pdf (accessed on 1 April 2016).

OECD (2016), 2015 OECD Recommendation of the Council on Gender Equality in Public Life, OECD Publishing, Paris, http://dx.doi.org/10.1787/9789264252820-en.

OECD (2015a), *All on Board: Making Inclusive Growth Happen*, OECD Publishing, Paris, http://dx.doi.org/10.1787/9789264218512-en.

OECD (2015b), *Policy Shaping and Policy Making: The Governance of Inclusive Growth*, www.oecd.org/governance/ministerial/the-governance-of-inclusive-growth.pdf (accessed on 1 April 2016).

OECD (2015c), "The OECD - A partner in open government". www.oecd.org/mena/governance/open-government.htm; www.slideshare.net/OECD-GOV/open-government-brochure.

OECD (2012), *OECD Territorial Reviews: The Chicago Tri-State Metropolitan Area, United States 2012*, OECD Publishing, Paris, http://dx.doi.org/10.1787/9789264170315-en.

Oxford University Press (2011), "Libya's Constitution of 2011", Constitute, www.constituteproject.org/constitution/Libya_2011.pdf (accessed on 1 April 2016).

Ruchti, Jefri J. (trans.) (2011), "Draft text of the Constitution adopted at the Referendum of 1 July 2011", HeinOnline World Constitutions Illustrated library 2011, www.constitutionnet.org/files/morocco_eng.pdf (accessed on 1 April 2016).

Senato della Repubblica (1947), Constitution of the Italian Republic, www.senato.it/documenti/repository/istituzione/costituzione_inglese.pdf (accessed on 1 April 2016).

The Palestinian Basic Law (2003), "2003 Permanent Constitution draft", www.palestinianbasiclaw.org/basic-law/2003-permanent-constitution-draft (accessed on 1 April 2016).

UK Government (2011), "Positive for Youth - A new approach to cross-government policy for young people aged 13 to 19", www.gov.uk/government/uploads/system/uploads/attachment_data/file/175496/DFE-00133-2011.pdf (accessed on 1 April 2016).

UNDP (trans.) (2014), "Tunisia's Constitution of 2014", Constitute, www.constituteproject.org/constitution/Tunisia_2014.pdf (accessed on 12 April 2016).

UNESCO (1998), "Lisbon Declaration on Youth Policies and Programmes", www.unesco.org/cpp/uk/declarations/lisbon.pdf (accessed on 12 April 2016).

United Nations (2007), "World Programme of Action for Youth", www.un.org/esa/socdev/unyin/documents/wpay2010.pdf (accessed on 1 April 2016).

Youthpolicy (2014), "1st Global Forum on Youth Policies, Report", 28-30 October 2014, Baku, Azerbaijan, www.youthpolicy.org/pdfs/GFYP_Report_20151015.pdf (accessed on 1 April 2016).

Youthpolicy.org (n.d.), "Factsheets", www.youthpolicy.org/factsheets (accessed on 12 April 2016)

Chapter 4

Open government: A lever to engage youth

Open government tools remain a fairly untapped opportunity to improve the context for youth to raise their voice and engage in public life. This chapter outlines pathways through which applying a youth perspective to open government tools can capitalise on young men and women's demand for having real impact in decision making.The chapter analyses how access to information, the creation of formal institutions for participation and new technologies can break down the barriers for young people to engage with their governments.

Open government tools and policies can be used to improve the context for young people to raise their voice and play a more active role in shaping decisions that affect their future. However, as of today, open government remains a fairly untapped opportunity to bring youth to the negotiating table.

If youth knew: Access to information policies

When young people have easy access to quality information they are better informed and can play a more active role in the public debate. Strong legal provisions and institutional capacities can make a significant difference in providing what youth hope is complete, objective, clear and reliable information. In turn, for policy makers to provide tailored solutions to the challenges faced by the younger generation, they need to rely on disaggregated and youth-specific data and information in various policy areas.

In most OECD countries, citizens enjoy a distinct right to access information. For this purpose, specific procedures have been established to regulate the proactive disclosure of information and the way information should be provided, among others (see Box 4.1).

Box 4.1. **An overview of access-to-information frameworks in OECD countries**

In 2011, 31 out of 34 OECD member countries had an access-to-information policy. In 25 countries, the policy covers information which is produced at the central and sub-national level. All countries oblige the executive to make information available while only 16 countries include the legislative and the judiciary. Private entities are covered by 18 countries.

The principle of maximum disclosure of information applies in all OECD countries. Exceptions are based on the class test (e.g. national security, international relations, personal data, commercial confidentiality, public order) or the harm test (e.g. persons, defence of state, commercial competitiveness). All OECD countries are publishing information proactively.

The right to know is ensured by provisions that guarantee the protection of the privacy, integrity, and anonymity of parties and individuals requesting information. In three out of four countries, civil servants have a formal duty to assist requestors. Less than half of all countries facilitate access for the disabled.

OECD countries offer multiple channels for citizens to submit requests (e.g. written/oral form, on line, via phone, in person) with standards in place to ensure a timely response (often 20 days). In around 25% of the countries, the information request is tracked on line and can be followed by the dispatcher.

Central online portals exist in 81% of OECD countries in parallel to other channels and online portals, such as the websites of individual ministries. Most OECD countries share an obligation that requires information to be published in re-usable formats.

Source: OECD (2011a), *Government at a Glance 2011*, OECD Publishing, Paris, http://dx.doi.org/10.1787/gov_glance-2011-en.

The right of young people to access information has been recognised in the Universal Declaration of Human Rights, the Convention on the Rights of the Child and the Convention for the Protection of Human Rights and Fundamental Freedoms. Recently, driven by the demand of youth and the aspiration of some MENA countries to deliver on the commitments made in the framework of the Open Government Partnership (OGP), the need to strengthen the respective legal and institutional frameworks has gained the attention of policy makers and non-governmental actors.

After having passed a decree law on access to administrative documents in 2011, Tunisia adopted an organic law on access to information in spring 2016. This law presents an important step for more transparency as it limits the exceptions to access to information and creates an access to information authority to support the effectiveness of the right. Morocco's constitution guarantees access to information. A draft law was adopted by its first Chamber (the Chamber of Representatives). To become effective it still has to be voted by the House of Councillors. In Jordan, an amendment to the 2012 law granted access to information to non-nationals. Jordan was the first country in the MENA region to enact the right to information if a legitimate reason exists, however, existing legislation such as the protection of state secrets and Documents Provisional Law can supersede the right.

The information young people request to manage key transitions in their lives can be distinct from information requested by the representatives of other age cohorts. They may wish to find information on school performance and education services, reproductive health, family planning and employment opportunities, to name but a few. The demand for youth-specific evidence is challenging policy makers to be responsive to it, in line with the good practice of many OECD countries in providing government services through a life events approach.[1]. Even less obvious areas can be of great interest to youth. Given the heavy impact of the allocation of state revenues on the availability and quality of public services information on youth-related expenditures should be accessible to increase accountability. For young people to be able to absorb this information and make effective use of it, it must be relevant, accurate, well communicated, and portrayed in a timely, easily understandable and accessible manner.

Policy makers in the MENA region should keep track of youth habits for accessing information to effectively reach out to them. With an increasing number of digital natives and an unprecedented uptake of mobile use, any government strategy should exploit the full range of information and communications technologies (ICTs). Obstacles to using ICT should be removed to avoid creating new divides. Traditional approaches, especially in remote rural and marginalised urban areas (e.g. roundtable discussions, counselling services), should complement more innovative forms of engagement. Recent initiatives use an explicit rights-based approach to advocate for young people's access to information. One example is the "Information Right Now!" campaign in Box 4.2.

Box 4.2. **The "Information Right Now!" campaign**

The Information Right Now! campaign was launched in 2012 by the European Youth Information and Counselling Agency (ERYICA) and the Council of Europe to promote a rights-based approach to ensure young people's access to information.

The campaign targeted young people, decision makers and the media throughout Europe to raise awareness among all stakeholders that youth indeed have a right to information. In Macedonia, youth and youth workers met with the presidents of the municipality councils; Croatia organised youth information fairs; and youth in Sweden gathered to celebrate the right to information in a street art festival.

Source: European Youth Information and Counselling Agency (2012), "Information Right Now!", www.informationrightnow.eu (accessed on 12 April 2016).

A second aspect that deserves the attention of policy makers and civil society is the paucity of youth-specific data.

Young people are by definition in a transitional period in their lives during which they move from school to work and leave their families to take their place as adults in society. Data must be sufficiently disaggregated to support conclusions about policy-relevant subgroups – the rich and the poor, men and women, rural and urban, educated and illiterate, able-bodied and the disabled – and to examine the interactions among these characteristic and the lives of the nation's youth. The integration of data plays a crucial role in this regard. Information on reproductive health issues, such as adolescent pregnancies, for example, if linked to information on workforce participation, schooling, income, and other social variables, could provide important elements to policy makers to effectively shape initiatives to target specific problems from a holistic perspective. Employment data should be brought together with educational, social, and income data to provide the basis for evidence-based policy making as well as assistance programmes.

The collaboration between Egypt's central statistical agency, CAPMAS, and the Population Council, a private research organisation, offers a good example of the type of cross-cutting analysis that can inform decision making with regard to youth (see Box 4.3). The Survey of Young People in Egypt (SYPE), first conducted in 2009, was repeated in 2014. It provides a detailed picture of how the economic, social, and attitudinal characteristics of young Egyptians have evolved over this five-year period.

Box 4.3. **Improving evidence for youth policy formulation: The Survey of Young People in Egypt**

The gap of detailed, comprehensive and reliable information for youth motivated the Population Council in Egypt to assemble a broad coalition of public and private institutions in 2006 to conduct what became the Survey of Young People in Egypt. SYPE undertook a nationwide survey of health, education, employment, international migration, marriage and family formation, social issues, values, civic engagement, time use, and attitudes toward gender roles.

SYPE adopted a design to capture variation within the youth population, including particular attention to incorporation of informal settlements (slums), which house a majority of Egypt's urban residents. Detailed, age-group-specific questionnaires including an aptitude test were administered to more than 15 000 youth. The sample was developed in close collaboration with Egypt's official census body, the Central Agency for Public Mobilisation and Statistics (CAPMAS). In addition to CAPMAS and the Population Council, SYPE engaged the National Center for Examinations and Educational Evaluation and the Information and Decision Support Center in the Prime Minister's office. SYPE's final report was issued in 2011, but SYPE data continue to be used for research and analysis both because the dataset is the most comprehensive one on the topic and because the Population Council has made the data available for any researcher to use.

SYPE has demonstrated its value for policy analysis and decision making through numerous studies and publications. The experience shows the value of taking a sufficiently broad approach to data collection to permit key relationships to be analysed, such as those between work and education, health and family life, and values and gender attitudes. It underscores the need to invest in data collection and the importance of mobilising a broad-based, public-private coalition of institutions to carry out the necessary comprehensive and large-scale analysis. The challenge is to institutionalise this type of data-driven work to permit it to be replicated as the basis for sound policy making and youth-responsive public governance.

The SYPE 2014 team was able to trace many of the participants in SYPE 2009, providing unique large-scale panel data that offer insights into how youth's lives have changed.

Source: Population Council West Asia and North Africa Office (2011), *Survey of Young People in Egypt: Final Report*, January; Dr. Ghada Barsoum, SYPE Principal Investigator, private communication, October 2014.

Set youth in motion: Opportunities and challenges for youth engagement

Providing systematic opportunities for citizens to engage is a fundamental component of open government strategies. It refers to the existence of formal and informal mechanisms for all segments of society to participate in the different stages of the policy-making cycle. Despite an unprecedented emergence of youth-driven and youth-focused associations in the region, capacity shortages and a general scepticism towards youth associations, present some of the obstacles to the successful organisation and mobilisation of youth interests (EuroMed, 2013).

Engagement can take different forms, such as proposing legislation, launching petitions and commenting on draft legislation through online or traditional consultations (OECD, 2015b). Specific measures designed to encourage young people to participate in these processes can lift some of the burden that discourages many from taking a more active stance. However, in many aspects, the political commitments for more open government in MENA countries still need to translate into opportunities that allow all segments of society, including youth, to get engaged on a broader scale.

Opportunities for youth to influence policy decisions can help legitimise the process and policies and provide a means for youth to hold government accountable (OECD, 2015c). OECD evidence suggests that expressing one's political voice and contributing to the political functioning of society is essential to individual well-being (OECD, 2011b). Furthermore, youth engagement in the MENA region allows young people to acquire individual skills, such as public speaking, agency and a sense for active citizenship and democratic principles. However, as one commentator convincingly argues "[b]y making the desired outcome individual improvement, rather than social change, we make every form of participation a success story while achieving very little in terms of political, social or economic change" (Farrow, 2015). Therefore, the intention of policy makers to strengthen youth skills is as important as pushing for institutional and legal reform to make the existing governance arrangements more youth-friendly.

A glance at youth engagement in MENA countries

In its most standard version, civic or political engagement is measured by looking at the turnout of voters. The OECD Better Life Index further incorporates the level of government transparency in the process of drafting legislation. Broader definitions refer to grass-root activities such as volunteering and attending public demonstrations and formal forms of engagement, for instance being a member in a civil society organisation or participating in public consultations.

This report embraces a broad definition of engagement. It takes into account the fact that traditional ways of participation in OECD and MENA countries are on the decline. Low turnout at national and local elections should not mislead policy makers to assume that the younger generation is disinterested in politics. Tech-savvy youth in the MENA region have made unprecedented use of social media, blogs, and other informal channels to raise their political voice, which fed into the civil uprisings that became known as the Arab Spring. It reflects that youth are a heterogeneous group with different socio-economic and cultural backgrounds as well as different preferences and means to engage with government. The case for a broader definition of participation has been made before by the Council of Europe's *Revised European Charter on the Participation of Young People in Local and Regional Life* (2013).[2]

Two recent studies underline the pertinence of looking at both formal and informal political activities. Both the 2014 SYPE study in Egypt and a targeted study of youth participation in Tunisia conducted by IWatch, a civil society organisation from Tunisia, found that, contrary to what many expected in the wake of the Arab Spring uprisings, MENA youth rarely choose traditional forms to participate in public life. Although they are among the active leaders in the region's leading civil society organisations, the IWatch survey found that only 5% are members of a political party and just 3% of them are active members . The results from this study are discussed in Box 4.4. SYPE found much lower levels in Egypt than those in Tunisia, with the share claiming membership in a political party, syndicate, NGO, or trade union falling below 1%. In Morocco, a 2012 survey carried out by the High Commission of the Plan revealed that only 6% of young people are members of a civil society association and that only 1.3% is affiliated to a political party or trade union (El Mnasfi, 2013).

Box 4.4. **Attitudes towards political engagement among Tunisian youth**

I Watch, a Tunisian civil society organisation, surveyed 600 Tunisian youth (aged 18-35) to measure their attitudes toward political participation and participatory democracy. Their overall findings underscore the weak connection to formal political activity among young Tunisians after the Jasmine Revolution. In the words of the study, "[t]hree years after the revolution, the Tunisian youth has little faith in politics as well as in political institutions." They found that youth were substantially more interested in informal mechanisms for participation, such as signing petitions, attending protests, or participating through social media, with almost two-thirds reporting having taken part in a protest during the past year.

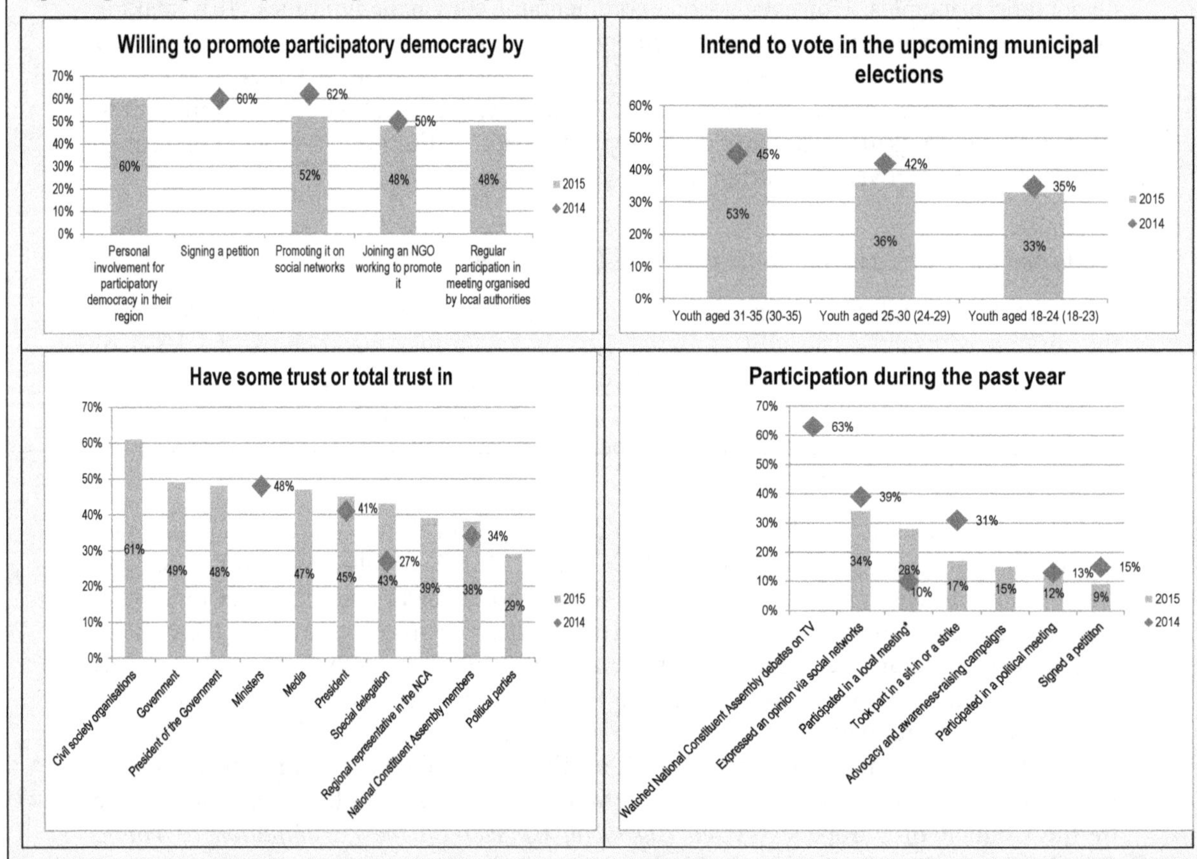

Box 4.4. **Attitudes towards political engagement among Tunisian youth** *(continued)*

Only a minority of youth reported that they planned to participate in the upcoming municipal elections. The survey data suggest, however, that interest in formal political participation through voting increases with age, at least within Tunisia's youth cohort. This finding is consistent with international experience. Recent data from the 2015 survey suggests that despite a few positive exceptions (e.g. youth participation in local meetings; trust in some of the public institutions), youth show decreasing levels of engagement in the categories covered by the report.

Source: I Watch (2014), "Survey on youth perceptions of participatory democracy", I Watch, Tunis; Ballingen, Julie (2002), "Youth voter turnout", in López Pintor, Rafael and Maria Gratschew (eds.), *Voter Turnout: A Global Report*, IDEA, Stockholm, pp. 111-114; I Watch (2015), Perception de la démocratie participative chez les jeunes Tunisiens, www.drive.google.com/file/d/0BxAb-uoXEIUtdnZxanpvYV9kWkU/view?pref=2&pli=1 (accessed on 10 April 2016).

These initial findings imply important policy implications, especially since other MENA countries do show similar participation patterns. For today's youth, using a mind-catching hashtag may have a quicker and more direct impact on mobilising their peers for a common cause than going through a political party which tends to be dominated by older cohorts. By addressing youth in networks where they feel comfortable expressing themselves, governments can reach out to those who are more reluctant or do not have the means to engage in formal processes. However, as final political decisions are being made in more formal arrangements, the appeal of traditional channels should increase by allowing youth a genuine say and impact in the process. Public officials should acquire the relevant skills to interact with youth in both online and offline networks. Clear communication guidelines as well as an upgrade of the technical and financial resources are critical to communicate how young people's ideas and feedback were taken into account to close the feedback loop.

The average active youth in MENA is male, well educated, informed and connected

To better understand existing divides in youth civic participation, Mercy Corps, a global humanitarian agency, conducted a study across MENA countries (Mercy Corps, 2012). In line with this report, the study assumes that the visibility of public activism among youth outside formal arrangements displays their frustration with the existing institutions and norms. Using data from the Arab Barometer, the study finds that the average activist is male, rather well educated, interested in politics, and regularly uses news and media sources, including the Internet, to obtain information.[3] The study concludes that household socio-economic status stands out as a major factor to determine the level of civic and political participation among youth in MENA.

What is "good" youth engagement?

Engagement differs in terms of the degree of formalisation (i.e. formalised versus informal ways), ownership (i.e. youth-driven versus government-driven approaches), scope (i.e. specific project versus long-term engagement or representation of youth needs) and thematic orientation. While this list of dimensions is not exhaustive it suggests that an evaluation of the quality of youth engagement eventually depends on the format and the expected outputs and impact.

The most well-known concepts to assess the quality of youth engagement are inspired by classic participation theories, such as Sherry Arnstein's Ladder of Citizen Participation (1969). Arnstein declares that citizen participation is citizen power and that, therefore:

> *"[i]t is the redistribution of power that enables the have-not citizens, presently excluded from the political and economic processes, to be deliberately included in the future. It is the strategy by which the have-nots join in determining how information is shared, goals and policies are set, tax resources are allocated, programs are operated, and benefits like contracts and patronage are parceled [sic!] out. In short, it is the means by which they can induce significant social reform which enables them to share in the benefits of the affluent society."*

Building on Arnstein's model, former UNICEF staff Roger Hart developed a ladder of children participation in the early 1990s, which is commonly referred to as the ladder of youth participation (Box 4.5). Hart argues that a nation is democratic to the extent that its citizens are involved, particularly at the community level. For him, citizen engagement is a learning process in which "[t]he confidence and competence to be involved must be gradually acquired through practice. It is for this reason that there should be gradually increasing opportunities for children to participate in any aspiring democracy, and particularly in those nations already convinced that they are democratic" (Hart, 1992). He concludes that despite opportunities for children and youth to participate in different degrees around the world, "it is often exploitative or frivolous".

Shier's Pathways to Participation (2001) (Figure 4.1) identifies five levels of participation. In the most rudimentary form, governments provide formal arrangements to listen to young people; the most advanced settings allow for an equal share of power and responsibility between youth and government officials in decision making. For each level, Shier identified three stages of commitment (e.g. openings, opportunities and obligations).

In line with the definition of "active participation" (as compared to information and consultation) by the OECD report "Citizens as Partners - Information, Consultation and Public Participation in Policy-Making" (2001), the two models outlined above stress the importance of a partnership approach between youth and the government, in which both sides share responsibilities and powers. Although the responsibility for the final decision or policy formulation rests with government, an equal standing in setting the agenda, proposing policy options and shaping the policy dialogue characterises advanced forms of engaging young men and women.

Box 4.5. **Reviewing the quality of youth participation: Hart's Ladder revised**

Hart's Ladder, as the model is referred to, is a seven-step scale to assess the degree of youth engagement in decision making. At the lowest step, adults/governments have complete and unchallenged authority and abuse their power ("manipulation") whereas youth are equal partners on the top of the ladder ("young people and adults share decision making"). It is evident that not every government project may be suitable for the highest level of youth involvement. As a first and crucial step, governments could aim for a minimum level of participation, characterised by overcoming the neglect of youth concerns or pseudo-forms of participation.

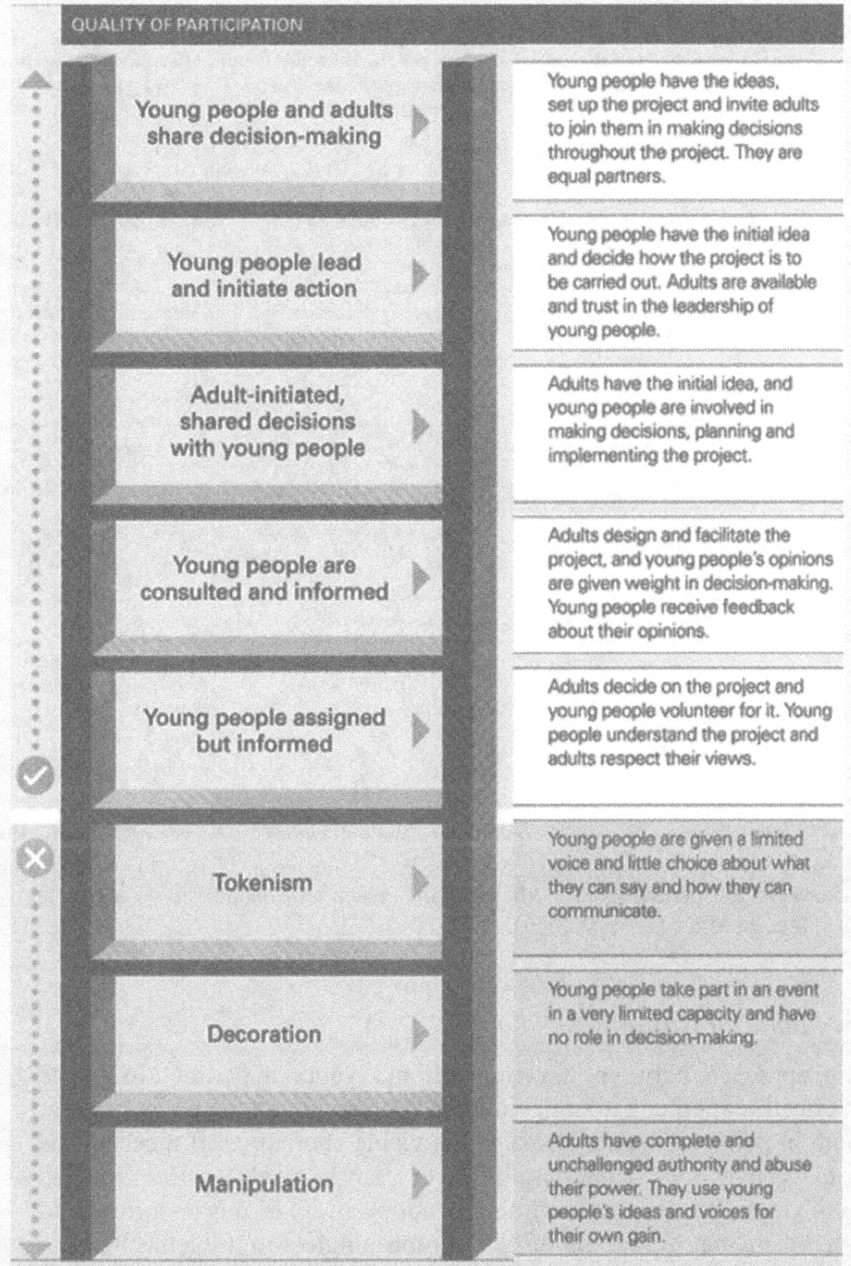

Source: Hart, Roger (1992), *Children's Participation from Tokenism to Citizenship*, UNICEF Innocenti Research Centre, Florence, http://www.unicef-irc.org/publications/pdf/childrens_participation.pdf; Government of New Zealand (n.d.a.), "Hart's Ladder", Ministry of Youth Development, www.myd.govt.nz/documents/engagement/harts-ladder.pdf (accessed on 1 April 2016).

Figure 4.1. **Shier's pathways to participation**

Shier's Pathways to Participation (2001)

LEVELS OF PARTICIPATION	OPENINGS	OPPORTUNITIES	OBLIGATIONS
Level 5 Young people share power and responsibility in decision-making.	Are you ready to share some of your adult power with young people?	Is there a procedure that enables young people and adults to share power and responsibility for decisions?	Is it a policy requirement that young people and adults share power and responsibility for decisions?
Level 4 Young people are involved in decision-making processes.	Are you ready to let young people join in your decision-making processes?	Is there a procedure that enables young people to join in decision-making processes?	Is it a policy requirement that young people must be involved in decision-making processes?
Shier states that level 3 of his model is the minimun practice needed to meet the requirements of the United Nations Convention on the Rights of the Child.			
Level 3 Young people's views are taken into account.	Are you ready to take young people's views into account?	Does your decision-making process enable you to take young people's views into account?	Is it a policy requirement that young people's views must be given weight in decision-making?
Level 2 Young people are supported in expressing their views.	Are you ready to support young people in expressing their views?	Do you have a range of ideas and activities to help young people express their views?	Is it a policy requirement that young people must be supported in expressing their views?
Level 1 Young people are listened to.	Are you ready to listen to young people?	Do you work in a way that enables you to listen to young people?	Is it a policy requirement that young people must be listened to?

Source: Shier, H. (2001), "Pathways to participation: Openings, opportunities and obligations", *Children and Society*, Vol. 15, John Wiley and Sons Ltd., pp. 107-117, www.ipkl.gu.se/digitalAssets/1429/1429848_shier2001.pdf; Government of New Zealand (n.d. b), "Shier's pathways to participation", Ministry of Youth Development, www.myd.govt.nz/documents/engagement/shier.pdf (accessed on 12 April 2016).

Involving youth in public consultations

A power-sharing approach between governments and youth may not always be feasible or the most effective approach to bring youth in. Depending on the policy issue at stake, involving youth in public consultations can be a viable alternative. If mechanisms to consult citizens exist in MENA countries, however, they typically suffer from an underrepresentation of youth. While many may simply not be aware of this opportunity to express their opinion, others may find it too difficult or meaningless to use a mechanism, which often comes without a clear follow-up procedure. If youth feel their input makes no difference to policy outcomes, they are unlikely to get involved. The MENA-OECD Practitioners' Guide for Engaging Stakeholders in the Rule-Making Process (2014a) provides useful guidance for governments to address frequent questions as to what form of consultation should be chosen, at what time and who should be involved.

Some notable initiatives have emerged over the past few years. In Northern Ireland, the Participation Network of Children in Northern Ireland (CiNI), formulated eight standards for policy makers and delivery units of public services for children and young people to increase their engagement. The "Ask First" standards, presented in Box 4.6., build on the input of children and young people, public sector personnel, the views of child and youth organisations and the Equality Commission for Northern Ireland Guidance for Public Authorities, and were endorsed by the Office of the First Minister and Deputy First Minister.

Box 4.6. **Standards for children and young people's participation in public decision making: "Ask First" standards in Northern Ireland**

- **A**ppropriate methods: Children and young people will be engaged in a variety of ways, based on what is best suited to their age and level of development/maturity. In particular, play-based methodologies will be developed for involving preschool children.
- **S**upport: Children and young people will be provided with the support needed to engage effectively in the decision-making process.
- **K**nowledge: Children and young people will be provided with the knowledge they need to engage fully in decision-making processes. Information will be easily understood, child-friendly and produced in a range of accessible formats.
- **F**eedback: Children and young people will be told about the outcomes of their involvement and how their input has been considered. Where their ideas have not been taken on board they will be told why this has happened.
- **I**nclusion: All children and young people will be facilitated to engage in public decision-making processes. Particular measures will be put in place to ensure the involvement of those who are vulnerable and marginalised, in line with Section 75 and UNCRC obligations.
- **R**espect: Children and young people will be treated with respect. They will decide the nature and extent of their involvement, including the option not to participate.
- **S**enior people: Children and young people will have direct contact with senior people who are in a position to make decisions and take action in relation to their ideas, views and experiences.
- **T**iming: Children and young people will be involved at the earliest possible stages of policy and service development, including processes to establish the need for service or policy initiatives.

Source: Summary taken from Leeson, Maurice (2014), "Involving disabled young people in the development of regional child and youth services", presentation at the UK Conference on Child Poverty and Well-being on 16 December 2014, Cardiff, www.childreninwales.org.uk/wp-content/uploads/2014/10/Maurice-Leeson.pdf (accessed on 1 April 2016).

Youth representative bodies: Youth councils, parliaments and fora

Outside the realms of government-driven consultation procedures, national youth councils (NYCs), youth parliaments and other youth-dedicated fora have emerged as a space for youth to express their opinion *vis-à-vis* government institutions. In almost all OECD member countries, NYCs or similar arrangements exist.

The mandate of national youth councils can vary considerably depending on the organisation and the degree to which they are independent from the government. While some NYCs are entirely youth-run and operate autonomously from government, such as in Belgium, Germany and Lithuania, NYCs in Costa Rica and the Philippines are integrated into the government structure. Whereas autonomous youth councils facilitate the co-ordination of national youth organisations, councils integrated into the government structure typically manage the state-youth relations (TakingITGlobal, 2006). While autonomous youth councils provide a national platform for youth organisations to more effectively represent youth concerns, integrated councils work as a link between youth organisations and the government with the aim of ensuring better communication and co-operation, more permanent youth participation and a smooth implementation of youth programmes. The influence over the decision-making process NYCs are able to exert thus varies. In the Slovak Republic, youth hold permanent seats in the Department of Youth of the Ministry of Education. In Latvia and Slovenia, NYCs were invited to write youth laws and hand them over to the parliament for approval. In OECD countries, NYCs have participated in monitoring the implementation of youth laws.

One of the most effective mechanisms for NYCs to shape policy outcomes exists in Lithuania (see Box 4.7).

In MENA countries, the Tunisian Young Parliaments and Lebanon´s Youth Forum for Youth Policy (see Box 4.8) curbed a space for active citizenship. Conversely, such interventions can be a barrier to progress if they are limited to token public relations activities or, most important, are presented as a solution to youth problems and therefore seen by the government as a substitute for tackling the structural barriers to youth engagement.

Box 4.7. **Lithuania Youth Council**

The Lithuania Youth Council (LiJOT), founded in September 1992 for the purpose of creating a co-ordinating structure to represent the interests of youth to the state, has gained recognition for establishing one of the most effective youth participation structures. After overcoming some initial challenges, such as obtaining legal recognition for youth policy and pushing for the Concept of State Youth Policy, LiJOT was successful in advocating the creation of a State Council for Youth Affairs, a body specifically responsible for youth affairs.

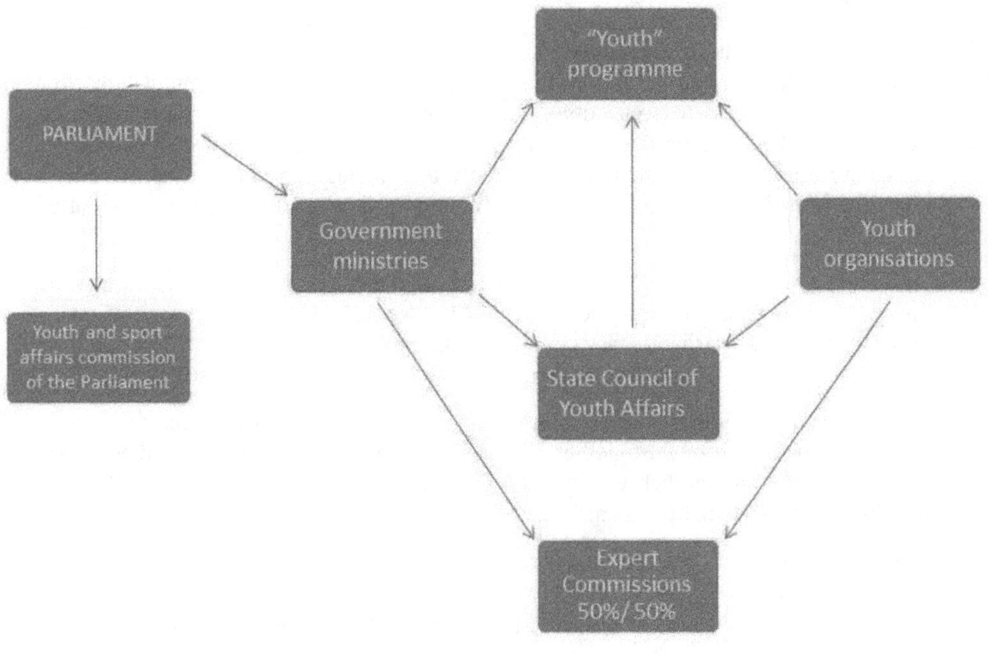

Based on the principle of "co-management" and "co-decision making", the State Council of Youth Affairs gathers an equal number of representatives from different ministries with a stake in youth-related issues upon the appointment by the Prime Minister and LiJOT. This permanent structure allows youth representatives to voice their concerns and take active part in decisions that affect youth policy and programmes.

Source: TakingITGlobal (2006) "National youth councils - Their creation, evolution, purpose, and governance", http://acdn.tigurl.org/images/resources/tool/docs/762.pdf (accessed on 10 April 2016); OECD's own work based on the Lithuania Youth Council.

Box 4.8. **Tunisian Young Parliaments and Lebanon's Youth Forum for Youth Policy**

Inspired by the European Youth Parliament – a European platform for political debate, intercultural encounters, civic education and the exchange of ideas among young people – the Tunisian civil society organisation Tun'Act organised the country's first Tunisian Young Parliaments in2013 and 2014. The Tunisian Young Parliaments have made an important contribution to providing a space to young people for embracing active citizenship and promoting a culture of democratic debate.

The Tunisian Young Parliaments brought together young men and women (aged 18-30) from different regions to gather in different thematic committees (e.g. environment, economy, international relations, social security and health, terrorism, culture, education, and human rights). Each commission was tasked with preparing a resolution in English, French or Arabic that was eventually adopted by vote. The participants were encouraged to give speeches, express personal opinions, and participate in voting procedures, which allowed them to acquire knowledge about the parliamentary process, foster respect for different opinions, strengthen teamwork and seek compromise. Many participants reportedly felt encouraged to be more active in civic, social and political life. The final resolution of the first Tunisian Young Parliament was brought to the attention of the party leaders.

The organisation of the third Tunisian Young Parliament is currently on hold due to a lack of long-term donor support. However, plans exist to strengthen mechanisms for follow-up on the conclusions, such as by discussing resolutions with relevant parliamentary committees in the future.

Similar efforts have been made in Lebanon. The Youth Forum for Youth Policy, a broad-based umbrella organisation of civil society and political parties' youth wings, manages five task forces that develop sectoral policy recommendations, which are brought together into an integrated policy document and are presented to the cabinet, most recently in 2011. An earlier example of good practice was the Youth Shadow Government, established by the Naharshabab Association, an affiliate of Nahar newspaper.

Starting in 2006, this programme brought together 30 youth leaders (one-third of whom were women) to form a shadow cabinet, with each person holding shadow ministry portfolios, reviewing government policies and promoting dialogue. It appears that the shadow ministry programme has not continued, however.

Source: Tun'Act (2016) http://tunact.org/; Youth Forum for Youth Policy (2016), www.youthforum-lb.org/en/ (accessed on 12 April 2016).

Recommendations

In line with the 2010 OECD Guiding Principles for Open and Inclusive Policy Making, MENA governments could encourage and build youth engagement in public life by:

1. **Promoting a whole-of-government approach**. Youth concerns are typically dealt with by a broad range of government units, therefore, strong horizontal and vertical communication and co-ordination mechanisms are critical to mainstream youth considerations in public policies and strategies and avoid fragmented delivery.

2. **Formulating national, integrated youth policies** in collaboration with youth associations, civil society organisations and activists outlining clear objectives, performance indicators, realistic timeframes and necessary financial, technical and human resources for effective and coherent youth programming across ministries and departments. While no single, unified framework exists to guide

the formulation, implementation and evaluation of youth policies, policy makers seeking guidance can consult the African Youth Charter (2006) and the Baku Commitment to Youth Policies (2014).

3. **Creating or strengthening the role of youth representative bodies (e.g. national/local youth councils) and allowing for new forms of youth engagement** (e.g. use of digital technologies) to engage youth across the policy cycle. In case a partnership approach of shared duties and responsibilities between youth and government representatives is not feasible but opportunities for public consultations exist, they should be designed such that young people feel encouraged to get involved. The MENA-OECD Practitioners' Guide for Engaging Stakeholders in the Rule-Making Process (2014a) provides useful guidance as governments are facing difficult choices with a view to the purpose and scope of youth consultation, the identification of youth representatives as well as the channels through which consultation can be most meaningful.
4. **Providing full access to information for youth**, especially in areas of particular importance to them (e.g. reproductive health, family planning, education services, employment opportunities, school performance). Active disclosure of information on the performance of government services is also of interest to youth and will strengthen accountability mechanisms. Data should be portrayed in an accessible, re-usable and easily understandable format (e.g. youth budget). Youth-led organisations can advise governments on the way information should be communicated and which channels should be used to make sure it is shared effectively. Governments should also consider establishing a regular cycle of sharing information using blogs, social media (e.g. Facebook, Google+, Twitter, Youtube podcasts) and mobile applications to inform youth about government programmes and solicit their views through feedback mechanisms.
5. **Collecting youth-disaggregated data** to tailor public policies and services to their needs. Ideally, data is sufficiently disaggregated to support conclusions about policy-relevant subgroups such as the rich and the poor, men and women, rural and urban youth, the educated and illiterate and the able-bodied and disabled.

Digital technologies as a potential "game changer" for inclusive policy making and service delivery

Previous chapters have already touched upon the potential of digital technologies to strengthen an inclusive approach to policy making. The 2014 OECD "Recommendation of the Council on Digital Government Strategies", calls on governments to use technologies for improving social inclusiveness, partnerships and government accountability. It acknowledges that the new digital environment offers opportunities for more collaborative and participatory relationships to shape political priorities and design and deliver public services through a partnership approach (e.g. citizen-driven approach). As youth are increasingly growing up as "digital natives",[4] social media and online networks may become a source for more regular youth-government interaction while open data may offer new economic opportunities for the tech-savvy generations.

A new generation of digital natives

In the context of a rapid expansion of Internet use and connectivity, new opportunities to access information, communicate and interact with public authorities are emerging. Internet use has been expanding at an average of 12.3% annually over the 2009-13 period in the selected MENA countries, led by increases of 17.9% in Egypt. Many more young people have become Internet users in the past five years (Figure 4.2).

Figure 4.2. **Internet use in selected MENA countries and Gulf Cooperation Council (GCC) country average, 2005, 2009 and 2013**

Percentage of adult population

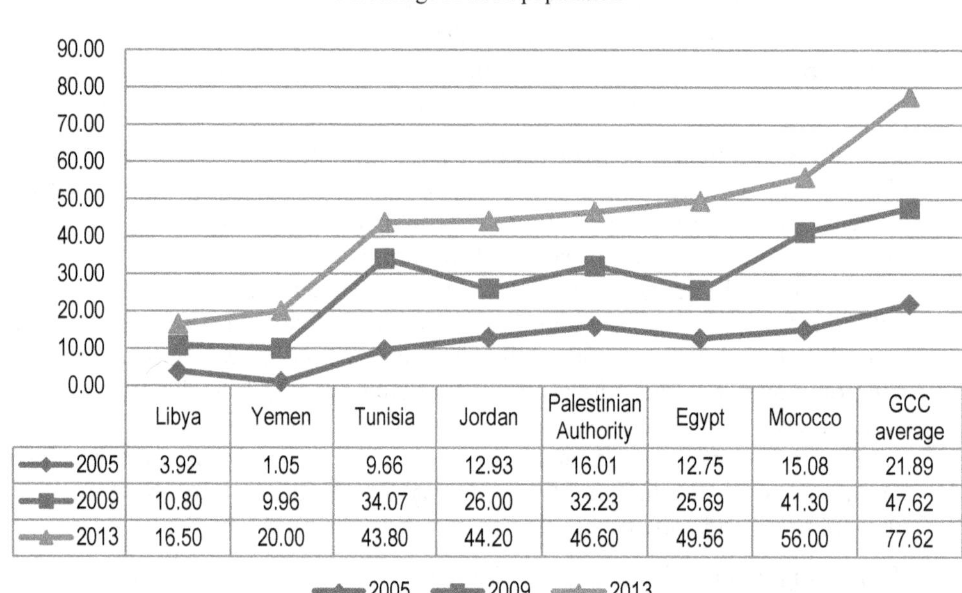

	Libya	Yemen	Tunisia	Jordan	Palestinian Authority	Egypt	Morocco	GCC average
2005	3.92	1.05	9.66	12.93	16.01	12.75	15.08	21.89
2009	10.80	9.96	34.07	26.00	32.23	25.69	41.30	47.62
2013	16.50	20.00	43.80	44.20	46.60	49.56	56.00	77.62

Source: World Telecommunication/ICT Indicators database (2016), http://www.itu.int/en/ITU-D/Statistics/Pages/publications/wtid.aspx (accessed on 1 April 2016).

The International Telecommunication Union (ITU) estimates the share of youth who can be classified as "digital natives". Table 4.1 presents the figures for 2013 and the unweighted average for GCC countries. Except for Libya and Yemen, more than one-third of young people in Egypt and Tunisia, and more than two-fifths of young men and women in Jordan and Morocco, are digital natives. While their share as part of the total population is still marginal, there is no doubt that future generations will increasingly use and request ICT solutions.[5]

Table 4.1. **Number of digital natives and as percentage of total and youth populations, 2013**

Rank	Country	Number of digital natives	Total population	Youth population (aged 15-24)
79	Egypt	5 532 746	6.6	34.9
55	Jordan	542 817	8.4	40.4
136	Libya	122 917	1.9	11.4
52	Morocco	2 829 799	8.7	45.8
81	Tunisia	700 044	6.5	36.7
127	Yemen	665 487	2.6	12.0
88	Total/average	10 393 810	5.8	30.2
73	GCC	4 952 201	7.0	47.8

Source: ITU (2013), *Measuring the Information Society*, ITU, Geneva, www.itu.int/en/ITU-D/Statistics/Documents/publications/mis2013/MIS2013_without_Annex_4.pdf (accessed on 2 April 2016).

The use of mobile devices has seen an even bigger surge over the recent years. In Yemen and the Palestinian Authority, 69 and 74 out 100 people, respectively, had mobile cellular subscriptions in 2013, compared to only 37 and 46, respectively, in 2009. In Libya, the number of mobile phones exceeds the total population (165 mobile cellular subscriptions per 100 people) (World Bank, 2013). However, sex-disaggregated data suggests that women are facing constraints in using the new digital tools and channels to the same degree men do (OECD, 2015b).

The widespread use of web 2.0 technologies and mobile devices has changed media behaviour in the Arab region. In a recent study with a focus on Egypt, Saudi Arabia and the United Arab Emirates, 35% of the respondents said they were following news by using online sources and portals. Some 30% rely on traditional media to follow the headlines and 28% on social media platforms (Mohammed Bin Rashid School of Government, 2014a).

The digital transformation is often referred to as a potential "game changer" for the interaction between governments and citizens. Indeed, the digital era introduces new channels and tools for government to inform (e.g. government websites, podcasts, RSS feeds), and interact with citizens (e.g. publication of draft regulation on line, surveys/consultation, e-petitions). The digitalisation of the public administration and related processes can reduce the costs and other barriers of public service use. As youth are typically among the first to exploit web-based channels, today's generation of digital natives can be a partner of government in designing user-friendly platforms.

Promising initiatives while significant challenges need to be overcome

MENA countries have stepped up efforts to increase their digital presence through government websites, online portals and experiments to consult with citizens on line. For instance, citizens in Jordan, Morocco and Tunisia were invited to comment on the draft access to information law. With a view to fighting corruption in public procurement, Tunisia developed the electronic procurement system TUNEPS with OECD support. Morocco established an online portal for whistleblowers to encourage the reporting of fraud and corruption. In Egypt, the Ministry of Communication and Information Technology established "IT clubs" in schools, universities and youth centres to provide open access to technology and ICT tools to low-income populations (OECD, 2013a). The

Court of Cassation has announced the design and implementation of an automated case management system to increase access to court data. With an update of the e-government policy strategy and the development of a medium-term implementation plan, the Palestinian Authority has laid the ground for a whole-of-government strategy to use ICT tools. Youth-led initiatives, such as Zabatak (www.zabatak.com) and HarassMap (www.harassmap.org) have become popular among young men and women for engaging users in reporting criminal activities and sexual harassment.

This progress has been reflected in the E-Government Development Index (EGDI) by the United Nations E-Government Survey 2014. The EGDI is a composite measure of three dimensions of e-government: telecommunication connectivity, human capacity and provision of online services. Due to significant advancement in each country studied in this report, they jumped from an average position of 131 (2012) to 98 (2014), out of 193 countries. The comparison of two of the above introduced indexes against the OECD average (see Figure 4.3) reveals that, while the study countries lag considerably behind in terms of available ICT infrastructure, countries like Jordan, Libya and Tunisia can rely on a rather well-educated and ICT-literate population.

Figure 4.3. **Comparison of selected MENA countries' scores based on the UN e-government indicators for ICT infrastructure and human capital, with the OECD average, 2014**

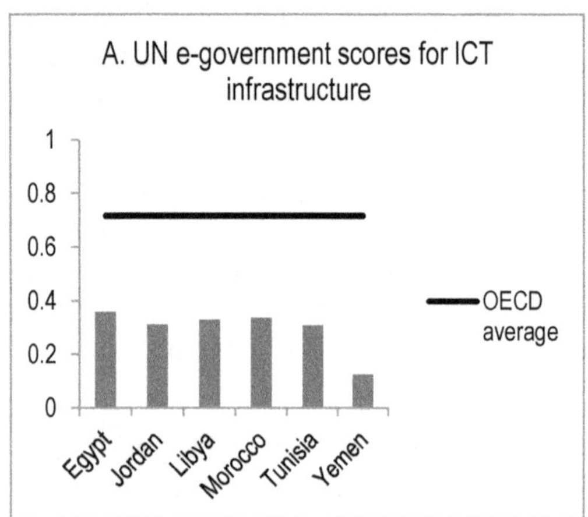

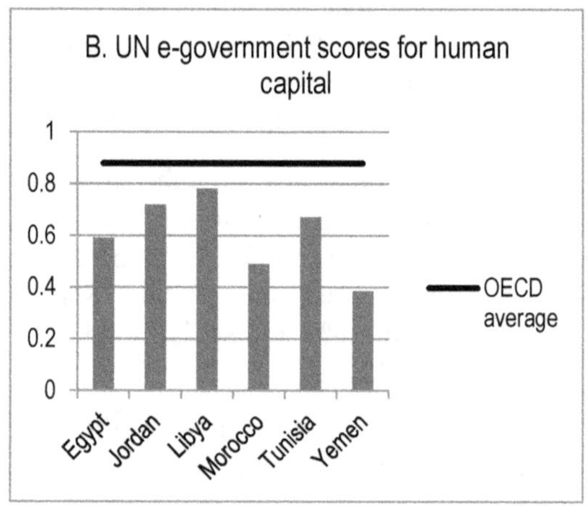

Note: The figure shows two composite indicators ranging from 0 to 1. Human capital is weighted by 2/3 adult literacy and 1/3 gross enrolment standard scores. The infrastructure index is a weighted average of standard scores on Internet users, mobile telephone subscriptions, telephone lines, fixed Internet subscriptions, and fixed broadband.

Source: UN (2014), *United Nations E-Government Development database*, http://unpan3.un.org/egovkb/en-us/Reports/UN-E-Government-Survey-2014.

Figure 4.4 compares the performance of selected MENA countries in using ICT to increase participation and deliver services against the OECD average. According the UN survey, Morocco ranks above the OECD average in the e-participation index while Tunisia follows closely behind. These results illustrate the successful steps made by both countries in recent years to provide public information and access to information online (e-information sharing) and, to a lesser degree, by offering a space where citizens can contribute to the deliberation on public policies and services (e-consultation). In Morocco, youth can find important information on the conditions and necessary documents related to marriage, pregnancy/giving birth, driver's license and the creation of an enterprise on the service portal of the government. It offers access to FAQs ("frequently asked questions" sections) and an opportunity to submit questions on line or through a call centre.

The OECD Open Government Reviews for Tunisia (2016) and Morocco (2015) find that e-consultation presents a largely untapped field in both countries and that a more structured and institutionalised approach was needed. More advanced interactions, such as submitting income taxes or registering for a business on line, will yet need to gain the full attention of public service providers to materialise. It should also be noted that the UN indicator does not provide information on the actual uptake of these opportunities by citizens.

The role of digital channels for civil society to inform, mobilise and co-ordinate initiatives is evident, not least since the civil uprisings for democratic reform that swept through some MENA countries. While many of the spontaneously founded networks disappeared, opengov.tn and tnOGP in Tunisia were established to strengthen the voice of civil society in the process of the country's membership in the Open Government Partnership. By reflecting a greater range of positions and interests and an enlarged geographic reach, the networks have strengthened the representativeness and credibility of CSOs in the consultation process for the country's OGP Action Plan.

Figure 4.4. **Comparison of selected MENA countries' scores based on the UN e-government indicators for online services and e-participation index, with the OECD average, 2014**

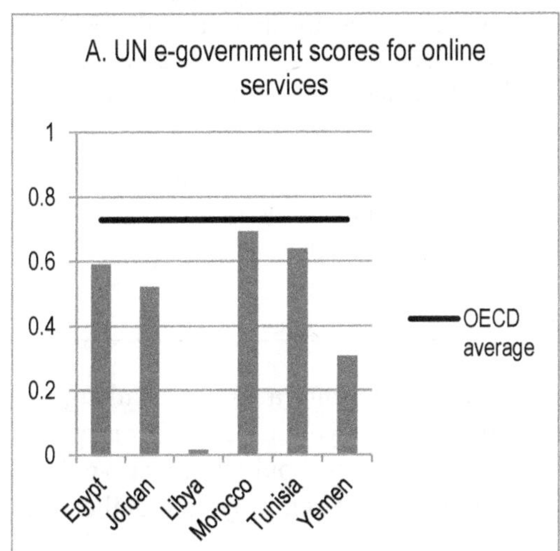

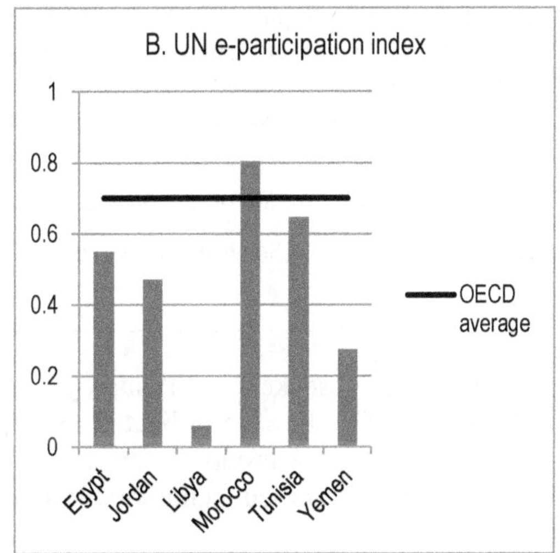

Note: The online services component assesses the technical features of national websites as well as e-government policies and strategies applied in general and by specific sectors for delivery of services. The e-participation index focuses on the use of online services to facilitate provision of information by governments to citizens ("e-information sharing"), interaction with stakeholders ("e-consultation") and engagement in decision-making processes ("e-decision making").

Source: UN (2014), *United Nations E-Government Development database*, http://unpan3.un.org/egovkb/en-us/Reports/UN-E-Government-Survey-2014.

A reality check in European countries demonstrates that simply putting up web-based content adds little to improve the interaction of youth with the public administration. Only 40% of young Europeans were using online services to interact with public authorities over the last year (Mickoleit, 2014). Large variations between individual countries (e.g. uptake rates vary between 20% in Italy and 70-80% in Slovenia, Iceland, Norway and Sweden) suggest, however, that countries with ICT-skilled public officials and capacities to design youth-tailored content are more successful in reaching out.

A glimpse into the potential of digital technologies for youth-tailored public policies and services

Over the last few years, OECD countries have made increasing use of online solutions to share information, consult with citizens and deliver public services. Although many government portals and websites still lack a youth-tailored presentation of information, the increasing expectation of young people to fill administrative documents on line and access relevant information with a simple click has led to the creation of new initiatives led by government, civil society and the private sector.

The South Australian consultation programme "YourSAy" (see Box 4.9) uses the Internet and in particular social media to involve citizens in public consultations. When the state reviewed its Strategic Plan for Development in 2010, "YourSAy" engaged local communities and citizens in discussions about environmental protection, housing provision, and, most notably, children and youth services.

Box 4.9. **YourSAy: Engaging youth in policy making in Australia**

What started as a simple experiment to engage young people at community level is now considered an important element of the policy-making process by the Government of South Australia. Today, more than 12 000 people are part of the online community, getting closer to 1% of the state's population. Through YourSAy, youth were recently invited to discuss the qualifications of a future Commissioner for Children and Young People, the state's Late Night Code following community concern about alcohol-fuelled incidents, and the governance arrangements in public schools and preschools.

YourSAy is very active on social media (e.g. Twitter, Facebook, LinkedIn, YouTube) where users can find information on upcoming consultations and youth-tailored surveys.

Source: Government of South Australia (2016), yourSAy, http://yoursay.sa.gov.au/ (accessed on 1 April 2016).

Matching jobseekers with employment opportunities presents a major challenge in MENA countries. Few co-ordinated services exist to facilitate young people's entry into the labour market. A group of young Palestinians partnered with Souktel, a tech venture, to create a mobile-based technology to bring youth and potential employers together (see Box 4.10).

Box 4.10. **JobMatch: A SMS-based job matching system in the Palestinian Authority**

JobMatch, uses a mobile-based technology developed by young Palestinians to close the job identification gap for unemployed youth not being reached by public employment services. It enables employers to post openings, receive applications, and make contact with jobseekers, who are able to search jobs, post brief resumes, and apply to listed positions. Souktel reports that their pilot programme in the Palestinian Authority was able to match an average of 40 youth/month with jobs or internships (approximately 500/year). Most matches were in sales, office support, information technology (IT), and construction and 7% of those matched were still in the positions at the three-month point. Youth reported a 75% reduction in the time needed to find a job, while employers reported halving the time and costs associated with hiring.

Box 4.10. JobMatch: A SMS-based job matching system in the Palestinian Authority *(continued)*

A study by Accenture and Vodafone found that "during the [Souktel JobMatch] pilot, 25% of users found roles, with the average job search reduced from 12 weeks to 1 week. Employers reported a 50% reduction in hiring time and 64% of workers reported an increase in salary." The Massachusetts Institute of Technology (MIT) also reported using Souktel to identify and hire hundreds of young Palestinians to participate in research projects.

It remains uncertain whether Souktel can establish the scale of operation to achieve financial sustainability beyond the donor-funded contracts that have thus far enabled it to grow. From its start-up in 2007, it has expanded to serve projects in 30 developing countries in the Middle East, Africa, Asia, and Latin America, enabling it to create a strong technical and business management team composed primarily of young Palestinians.

Source: Global Business School Network (2014), "Souktel and MIT bring digital outsourcing work to youth in Palestine, via mobile," 23 April, www.gbsnonline.org/blogpost/760188/186221/Souktel-and-MIT-Bring-Digital-Outsourcing-Work-To-Youth-in-Palestine-Via-Mobile; Souktel (2009), "Souktel: Mobile technology that helps youth find jobs and training", PowerPoint presentation, December; Vodafone (2013), "Connected worker: How mobile technology can improve working life in emerging economies", April, https://www.vodafone.com/content/dam/vodafone-images/sustainability/downloads/vodafone_connected_worker.pdf (accessed on 1 April 2016).

While youth are less likely to be involved in legal controversies than adults, they can be particularly vulnerable as they struggle to find information about their rights and legal advice. YouthLaw Aetearoa, a New Zealand-based project, addressed this challenge by providing free legal counsel to youth on line (see Box 4.11).

Box 4.11. New Zealand: Free legal online services for children and young people

YouthLaw is a free community law centre for children and young people across New Zealand. It provides free legal services to anyone below 25 who is unable to access legal help elsewhere. YouthLaw is primarily funded by the Ministry of Justice, but is independent of the government.

YouthLaw publishes legal information and education on a website and social media (www.facebook.com/YouthLaw) and provides legal advice offline (e.g. nation-wide free legal advice over the phone). The website covers areas of particular relevance to youth, such as home and family, relationships, school, shops and purchases, health and well-being, police and courts, driving, work, flatting, bullying and violence, welfare and benefits, and human rights. In the harassment section, for instance, the website explains what kind of behaviour is considered harassment and provides both concrete examples and links to the relevant laws and regulations.

Through interactive workshops in the offline world, YouthLaw has contributed to raise awareness among youth, associations and teachers for young people's rights and the importance of rights-based education.

Source: YouthLaw Aoearoa (2016) www.youthlaw.co.nz/ (accessed on 23 March 2016).

Social media and open government data: Potential for new forms of interaction and economic opportunities

In 2014, an estimated 81 million people in the Arab world used Facebook, up from 54.5 million just a year before. As shown in Figure 4.5, youth constitute around two-thirds or more of all Facebook users in the selected MENA countries. In line with the findings of the uptake rates on mobile phones, however, young women are significantly under-represented. The use of LinkedIn, a network system for professionals, is lower, but rising quickly. Moreover, Twitter is increasingly used as a communication tool with around 5.8 million active users, with the highest penetration rates reached in Egypt, Jordan and the Palestinian Authority (Mohammed Bin Rashid School of Government, 2014b).

Figure 4.5. **Youth social media use in selected MENA countries, 2014**

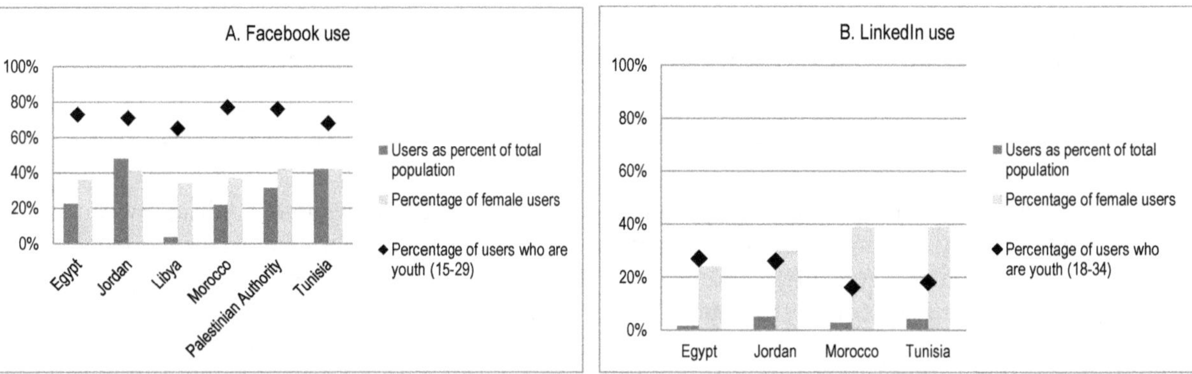

Note: Panel A refers to youth as young people between the ages of 15-29, whereas Panel B refers to young men and women between the ages of 18-34. No information is available for Libya and the Palestinian Authority for Panel B.

Source: Mohammed Bin Rashid School of Government (2014b), "Citizen engagement and public services in the Arab world: The potential of social media", 6th edition, June, www.mbrsg.ae/getattachment/e9ea2ac8-13dd-4cd7-9104-b8f1f405cab3/Citizen-Engagement-and-Public-Services-in-the-Arab.aspx (accessed on 1 April 2016).

Social media and mobile apps are essential tools in young peoples' lives to connect with friends and make sense of the world. They provide an easy-to-access space to seek information and advice, dialogue, or simply entertainment and distraction. Social media platforms like Facebook, Twitter, YouTube, Flickr, Instagram, MySpace and Tumblr pick up on the desire of young people to socialise and participate in viral activities by allowing them to build their own online communities and share interests with like-minded fellows. In both MENA and OECD countries, social media provide a space to exchange advice on taboo themes in society (e.g. sexuality, mental health) and hence presents an important source for young men and women to establish contacts and foster mutual encouragement (Youth Affairs Council of Victoria, 2013). Online blogs cover all parts of youth life and have been crucial to voice opinions and mobilise for common causes. Young people have been using social media to create social and political change during the Arab Spring, in Brazil prior to the World Cup, in the Occupy Wall Street Movement and during the Taksim Square Protests in Turkey (Smith, 2013). And yet, the new (mobile) technology is still unaffordable for a significant part of the younger generation which puts them at risk of social exclusion.

In the formulation of policies and the design of public services, governments need to take the new realities into account, simply because the online sphere is the place where young people mingle and seek information. If social media can encourage young people with little interest in participating through traditional channels, or if the online networks rather provide another pitch for the already active ones, however, is a matter of ongoing debate (Livingstone, Couldry and Markham, 2007).

Many civil society organisations in the Middle East and North Africa rely on a Facebook page instead of a more formal website given the ease of use which is free of charge and offers a form of two-way communication. Hundreds of informal youth groups were active on Facebook in Egypt and other MENA countries in the months following the January 2011 uprising, using their pages to organise protests, mobilise for local initiatives, and communicate on political developments, as well as for social purposes (Bremer, 2011). However, the reality check of social media use in Europe shows that while 85% of 16-24 year-old Europeans on average used social media in 2014, less than one-fifth used it to discuss political or civic issues (Figure 4.6).

Figure 4.6. **Youth social media use: General vs. political/civic issues, 2013**

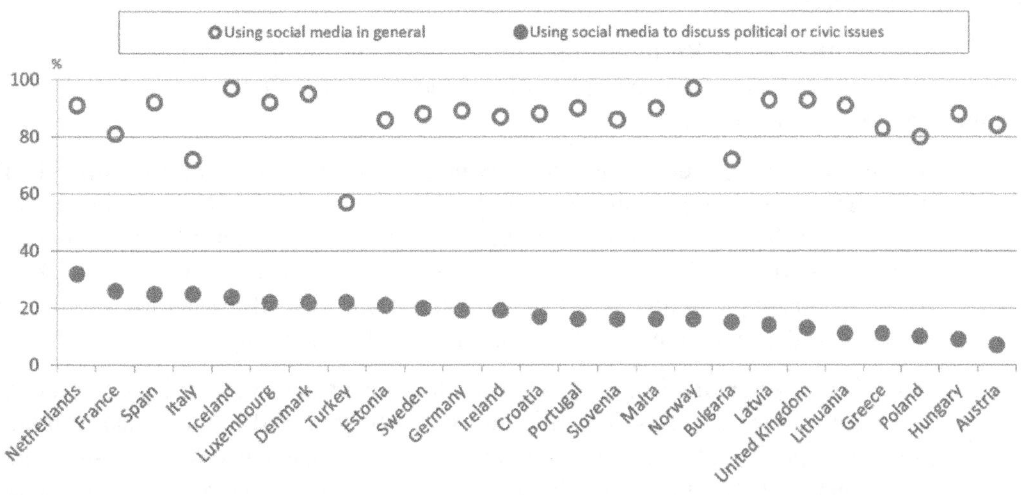

Source: Mickoleit, A. (2014), "Social media use by governments: A policy primer to discuss trends, identify policy opportunities and guide decision makers", *OECD Working Papers on Public Governance*, No. 26, OECD Publishing, http://dx.doi.org/10.1787/5jxrcmghmk0s-en.

In line with the trend in European countries, a recent study finds that almost half of young people in MENA countries do not use their accounts to discuss government performance. Those who do use social media to access government information (75%) whereas only a minority provides feedback (10%) and suggestions for improvements (7.5%) or communicates directly with senior government officials (5%) (Mohammed Bin Rashid School of Government, 2014b). According to another study targeting residents of 22 Arab countries, only 7% use social networking websites primarily to contribute to the community and society and less than 5% to share opinions and inform about political activities. Instead, the main use of social media was dedicated toget news, information and advice (27%), to stay in touch with family and friends (27%) and to find a job, freelancing and consulting opportunities (14%) (Mohammed Bin Rashid School of Government, 2014a). These findings point to the importance for governments to clearly define the purpose of their social media initiatives with effective follow-up and feedback mechanisms in place. The latter is particularly important as frustration can grow when youth feel that their input is not taken into account. Moreover, too many government websites bear the signature of public officials with little expertise in presenting information to distinct audiences. Governments can increase the appeal of their digital presence by partnering with young IT experts.

Beyond the positive impact of open data on transparency, accountability and public engagement (Ubaldi, 2013), access to government data and databases (e.g. legal information, business information or social data) can spur innovation and encourage the creation value-added services in collaboration with government. In Canada, Niew Labs, a group of graduated engineers and developers from the University of Toronto, designed "CareerPath" (Niew Labs, 2016). CareerPath, which can be accessed via a website and a mobile app, allows Canadian youth to search 40 000 job titles and view visualisations of projected employment statistics and job prospects based on data from Employment and Social Development Canada. The service ties the user's research to actual job opportunities and hence provides helpful advice to young jobseekers.

Recommendations

In line with the OECD Recommendation on Digital Government Strategies, MENA governments could exploit the potential of digital technologies to engage youth and tailor public services to youth needs by:

1. **Strengthening governance frameworks to further build up ICT infrastructure** as it presents one of the areas in which MENA countries lack considerably behind the OECD average. In light of the existing "digital divide", which puts vulnerable youth (e.g. women, rural, poor) at a significant risk of social exclusion, initiatives to build up the technical infrastructure should be sensitive to the specific needs and requirements of these groups.
2. **Investing in the skills of public officials** to interact with youth via social media and other online platforms. The trainings could be included in the annual training plans for public officials and involve youth representatives to ensure that government information is provided in a way that young people find appealing. Social media engagement could be embedded into the description of job positions and work plans to ensure that adequate time, capacities and resources are allocated to this task.
3. **Conducting an analysis of public services of particular interest to youth** that could be made available on line at low cost and with relatively little effort, such as free legal counsel.
4. **Strengthening the use of ICT-based methods to expand consultation with youth**, including online user surveys or opinion research and new forms of interaction via social media. Governments should complement online activities with more traditional forms of interaction (e.g. roundtables) to make sure that youth without access to digital technologies can raise their voice and contribute to the decision-making process. Through feedback mechanisms, the participants should be informed about how their input was taken into account.
5. **Investigating the reasons for the existing gender gap in using digital technologies** to provide similar opportunities for men and women.

6. **Using mobile technologies to facilitate the matching of job applicants with employers** and other forms of promoting youth participation in economic life as demonstrated by Souktel in Jordan, the Palestinian Authority, and elsewhere (see Box 4.10).

Notes

1. See www.digitalgov.gov/2015/05/15/government-services-through-a-life-events-approach/.
2. The *Revised European Charter on the Participation of Young People in Local and Regional Life* states: "Young people have the right and should have the opportunity to have a real say when decisions affecting them are being made at local and regional level. They should also be supported and given the space to be involved in all kinds of activities and actions."
3. The Arab Barometer is a multi-country survey designed to assess citizen attitudes about public affairs, governance, and social policy in the Arab world, and to identify factors that shape these attitudes and values. Its objective is to produce scientifically reliable data on the politically relevant attitudes of ordinary citizens, to disseminate and apply survey findings in order to contribute to political reform, and to strengthen institutional capacity for public opinion research (www.arabbarometer.org/).
4. "Digital natives" refers to youth who have been using the Internet for at least five years, according to the definition of the ITU.
5. It should also be noted that these estimates naturally underestimate the number of youth with Internet experience, because they exclude young people with less than five years of such experience.

References

Arab Barometer (2016), www.arabbarometer.org/ (accessed on 1 April 2016).

Arnstein, Sherry (1969), "A ladder of citizen participation," *Journal of American Planning*, Vol. 35, No. 4, pp. 216-224.

Ballingen, Julie (2002), "Youth voter turnout", in López Pintor, Rafael and Maria Gratschew (eds.), *Voter Turnout: A Global Report*, IDEA, Stockholm, pp. 111-114.

Bremer, Jennifer (2011), "Leadership and collective action in Egypt's popular committees: Emergence of authentic civic activism in the absence of the state," *International Journal of Not-for-Profit Law* 13 (4), December, pp. 70-92.

Council of Europe (2013), *Revised European Charter on the Participation of Young People in Local and Regional Life*, www.coe.int/t/dg4/youth/Source/Resources/PR_material/2015_Brochure_Youth_Participation_Charter_web_ENG.pdf (accessed on 1 April 2016).

El Mnasfi, Mustapha (2013), *Les jeunes au Maroc, entre exclusion et absence de confiance*, www.medea.be/2013/12/les-jeunes-au-maroc-entre-exclusion-et-absence-de-confiance/ (accessed on 1 April 2016).

EuroMed (2013), *Le travail de jeunesse en Tunisie après la révolution*, September, http://euromedyouth.net/IMG/pdf/tunisie_apre_s_re_volution_fr.pdf_02-09-13_def.pdf (accessed on 1 April 2016).

European Youth Information and Counselling Agency (2012), "Information Right Now!", www.informationrightnow.eu (accessed on 12 April 2016).

Farrow, Alex (2015), "Participation in 2015: A positive explosion of youth or a struggle to stay relevant?", 7 April, www.youthpolicy.org/blog/participation-global-governance/participation-struggling-to-stay-relevant/ (accessed on 10 April 2016).

Global Business School Network (2014), "Souktel and MIT bring digital outsourcing work to youth in Palestine, via mobile," 23 April, www.gbsnonline.org/blogpost/760188/186221/Souktel-and-MIT-Bring-Digital-Outsourcing-Work-To-Youth-in-Palestine-Via-Mobile (accessed on 1 April 2016).

Government of New Zealand (n.d.a.), "Hart's Ladder", Ministry of Youth Development, www.myd.govt.nz/documents/engagement/harts-ladder.pdf (accessed on 1 April 2016).

Government of New Zealand (n.d.b.), "Shier's pathways to participation", Ministry of Youth Development, www.myd.govt.nz/documents/engagement/shier.pdf (accessed on 12 April 2016).

Government of South Australia (2016), "yourSAy", http://yoursay.sa.gov.au/ (accessed on 1 April 2016).

Hart, Roger (1992), *Children's Participation from Tokenism to Citizenship*, UNICEF Innocenti Research Centre, Florence, http://www.unicef-irc.org/publications/pdf/childrens_participation.pdf (accessed on 1 April 2016).

ITU (International Telecommunication Union) (2013), *Measuring the Information Society*, ITU, Geneva, www.itu.int/en/ITU-D/Statistics/Documents/publications/mis2013/MIS2013_without_Annex_4.pdf (accessed on 2 April 2016).

I Watch (2015), Perception de la démocratie participative chez les jeunes Tunisiens, www.drive.google.com/file/d/0BxAb-uoXEIUtdnZxanpvYV9kWkU/view?pref=2&pli=1 (accessed on 10 April 2016).

I Watch (2014), "Survey on youth perceptions of participatory democracy", I Watch, Tunis.

Leeson, Maurice (2014), "Involving disabled young people in the development of regional child and youth services", presentation at the UK Conference on Child

Poverty and Well-being on 16 December 2014, Cardiff, www.childreninwales.org.uk/wp-content/uploads/2014/10/Maurice-Leeson.pdf (accessed on 1 April 2016).

Livingstone, S., N. Couldry and T. Markham (2007), "Youthful steps towards civic participation: Does the Internet help?", in Loader, B. (ed.), *Young Citizens in the Digital Age: Political Engagement, Young People and New Media,* Routledge, London, pp. 21-34.

Mercy Corps (2012), "Civic engagement of youth in the Middle East and North Africa: An analysis of key drivers and outcomes", March, www.mercycorps.org/sites/default/files/mena_youth_civic_engagement_study_-_final.pdf (accessed on 1 April 2016).

Mickoleit, A. (2014), "Social media use by governments: A policy primer to discuss trends, identify policy opportunities and guide decision makers", *OECD Working Papers on Public Governance*, No. 26, OECD Publishing, http://dx.doi.org/10.1787/5jxrcmghmk0s-en.

Mohammed Bin Rashid School of Government (2014a), "The Arab world online 2014: Trends in Internet and mobile usage in the Arab region", www.mbrsg.ae/getattachment/ff70c2c5-0fce-405d-b23f-93c198d4ca44/The-Arab-World-Online-2014-Trends-in-Internet-and.aspx (accessed on 1 April 2016).

Mohammed Bin Rashid School of Government (2014b), "Citizen engagement and public services in the Arab world: The potential of social media", 6th edition, June, www.mbrsg.ae/getattachment/e9ea2ac8-13dd-4cd7-9104-b8f1f405cab3/Citizen-Engagement-and-Public-Services-in-the-Arab.aspx (accessed on 1 April 2016).

Monroe, Mary Ann (2015), Government services through a life events approach, (15 May 2015), www.digitalgov.gov/2015/05/15/government-services-through-a-life-events-approach/ (accessed on 1 April 2016).

Niew Labs (2016), "Career Path", http://niewlabs.github.io/careerPath/#/home (accessed on 1 April 2016).

OECD (2016), *Open Government in Tunisia*, OECD Public Governance Reviews, OECD Publishing, Paris, http://dx.doi.org/10.1787/9789264227118-en.

OECD (2015a), *Open Government in Morocco,* OECD Public Governance Reviews, OECD Publishing, Paris, http://dx.doi.org/10.1787/9789264226685-en.

OECD (2015b), "The OECD - A partner in open government", www.oecd.org/mena/governance/open-government.htm; www.slideshare.net/OECD-GOV/open-government-brochure (accessed on 1 April 2016).

OECD (2015c), *All on Board: Making Inclusive Growth Happen*, OECD Publishing, Paris, http://dx.doi.org/10.1787/9789264218512-en.

OECD (2014a), *MENA-OECD Practitioners' Guide for Engaging Stakeholders in the Rule-Making Process*.

OECD (2014b), Recommendation of the Council on Digital Government Strategies, www.oecd.org/gov/digital-government/Recommendation-digital-government-strategies.pdf (accessed on 1 April 2016).

OECD (2013), OECD e-Government Studies: Egypt 2012, OECD Publishing. http://dx.doi.org/10.1787/9789264178786-en.

OECD (2011a), *Government at a Glance 2011*, OECD Publishing, Paris, http://dx.doi.org/10.1787/gov_glance-2011-en.

OECD (2011b), *How's Life?: Measuring Well-being*, OECD Publishing, Paris, http://dx.doi.org/10.1787/9789264121164-en.

OECD (2010), OECD Guiding Principles for Open and Inclusive Policy Making, www.oecd.org/gov/42370872.pdf.

OECD (2001), *Citizens as Partners: Information, Consultation and Public Participation in Policy-Making*, OECD Publishing, Paris, http://dx.doi.org/10.1787/9789264195561-en.

Population Council West Asia and North Africa Office (2011), *Survey of Young People in Egypt: Final Report*, January.

Shier, H. (2001), "Pathways to participation: Openings, opportunities and obligations", *Children and Society*, Vol. 15, John Wiley and Sons Ltd., pp. 107-117, www.ipkl.gu.se/digitalAssets/1429/1429848_shier2001.pdf (accessed on 1 April 2016).

Smith, Brittany (2013), "Tips for youth engagement on social media", *Build social*, 7 August, www.buildsocialconsulting.com/youth-engagement-social-media/.

Souktel (2009), "Souktel: Mobile technology that helps youth find jobs and training", PowerPoint presentation, December.

TakingITGlobal (2006), "National youth councils - Their creation, evolution, purpose, and governance", http://acdn.tigurl.org/images/resources/tool/docs/762.pdf (accessed on 10 April 2016).

Tun'Act (2016), http://tunact.org/ (accessed on 12 April 2016).

Ubaldi, B. (2013), "Open government data: Towards empirical analysis of open government data initiatives", *OECD Working Papers on Public Governance*, No. 22, OECD Publishing, http://dx.doi.org/10.1787/5k46bj4f03s7-en.

UN (United Nations) (2014), *United Nations E-Government Development database*, http://unpan3.un.org/egovkb/en-us/Reports/UN-E-Government-Survey-2014 (accessed on 1 April 2016).

Vodafone (2013), "Connected worker: How mobile technology can improve working life in emerging economies", April, https://www.vodafone.com/content/dam/vodafone-images/sustainability/downloads/vodafone_connected_worker.pdf (accessed on 1 April 2016).

Youth Affairs Council of Victoria (2013), "'What makes you tweet?' Young people's perspectives on the use of social media as an engagement tool", www.yacvic.org.au/component/docman/doc_download/336-report-what-makes-you-tweet-young-people-s-perspectives-on-the-use-of-social-media-as-an-engagement-tool (accessed on 1 April 2016).

Youth Forum for Youth Policy (2016), www.youthforum-lb.org/en/ (accessed on 1 April 2016).

YouthLaw Aoearoa (2016), www.youthlaw.co.nz/ (accessed on 23 March 2016).

World Bank (2013), "Mobile cellular subscriptions (per 100 people) in 2013", *World Development Indicators*.

World Telecommunication/ICT Indicators database (2016), http://www.itu.int/en/ITU-D/Statistics/Pages/publications/wtid.aspx (accessed on 1 April 2016).

Chapter 5

Mainstreaming youth considerations in public governance

This chapter draws attention to the critical role public governance plays for setting the conditions for young men and women to raise their voice and engage in policy making. Noting that the considerations of young men and women in MENA are insufficiently reflected in public policies and strategies, and the delivery of public services, the chapter introduces pathways through which governments can work towards mainstreaming youth considerations. It argues that the integration of youth in public governance – the system of strategic processes and tools, as well as institutions, rules and interactions for effective policy making – is key to readjust them towards youth needs and increase the impact of youth programming. This concept is discussed with a view to the following fields: public sector integrity, public budgeting, public human resource management, regulatory policy, local governance and gender equality.

Public sector integrity: Secure a fair youth share of public resources

The trust of citizens in public institutions and government has eroded in both OECD and Middle East and North Africa (MENA) countries. Youth trust in government is no exception. As shown by Figure 3.1 in Chapter 3, the trust of the younger generation in the abilities of the government to respond to their needs is considerably lower than among their parents across all MENA countries covered in this report.

OECD evidence suggests that the degree of public sector integrity is a crucial determinant of trust.[1] Integrity policies and institutions with strong mandates to scrutinise government action can increase the credibility and legitimacy of policy makers, safeguard the public interest and restore confidence. The link between young people's trust in public institutions and in their own future, economic growth and social progress has been highlighted by the OECD.[2] If regaining youth trust in government through improved integrity frameworks is a matter of urgency for OECD countries, it is even more acute for MENA countries. In the 2014 Corruption Perceptions Index of Transparency International, no country covered in this report is ranked among the first 50 (out of 175). Jordan still does comparatively well at 55th position, whereas Libya is placed among the ten countries with the lowest score (Transparency International, 2014a).[3]

How does corruption affect youth in MENA countries?

Youth in MENA countries are affected by corruption through at least three pathways. First, they encounter corruption in their interaction with public institutions and officials hence undercutting the quality of services and reducing the creation of jobs. Second, petty corruption is an endemic phenomenon in MENA countries. Finally, young people suffer from political corruption that diverts resources and power away from effective use and opportunities. Each dimension will be discussed below.

Youth play specific roles in society, as students, workers, customers, or voters, all of which present potential entry points for those seeking undue influence. The OECD Integrity Review of Tunisia underlines that the risk of corruption is particularly high in the delivery of social services on which many young men and women rely. Youth are the primary users of secondary and tertiary education and among the main users of health services, job placement and employment bureaus. Each of these activities is vulnerable to corruption which can take the form of informal payments, bribery or disguised corruption, such as private lessons in secondary education and faculty sale of unpublished textbooks in university courses. The lack of accountability mechanisms in education contributes to such deleterious practices as cheating and side payments in tertiary education or teacher absence. The OECD Integrity scan of Tunisia found that 70% of 15-year-old secondary school students in Tunisia participate in lessons outside of their classrooms to succeed in school (OECD CleanGovBiz, 2013). This shift points to quality deficiencies in schooling systems, but it is also linked to a more general lack of confidence in public institutions.

Petty corruption presents another enormous problem with detrimental effects on youth. In a society where the success of (commercial) interactions, the reception of official documents (e.g. driving licenses) and the access to public services depends on the payment of additional charges, it is hard to imagine how things could work otherwise. Petty corruption is an enormous, but largely trivialised problem as a study conducted by the Tunisian Association of Public Controllers, a civil society organisation, confirms. In this study, 70% of interviewees think that petty corruption facilitates daily interactions. This opinion is particularly popular among the younger cohorts (aged 18-25) of which 75% agree with that statement *vis-à-vis* 63% of those 55 years or older (Association Tunisienne des Contrôleurs Publics, 2015).

Finally, youth suffer from the distorting effects of corruption in public decision making. It diverts public money and influence away from the centre of society and cuts funding to improve education and health services, job opportunities and other critical services for youth. For example, when public construction costs are inflated, fewer new schools are built and young populations remain under-served, particularly in fast-growing peri-urban areas. A policy note prepared for the World Bank's 2005 Egypt Public Expenditure Review found that schools constructed by the state's General Authority for Educational Buildings "cost as much as 46.5% more for primary and preparatory schools and 15.9% more for secondary schools" than comparable schools built by an international non-governmental organisation (NGO) with donor funds (World Bank, 2005).

Involve youth in strengthening public sector integrity

Governments can partner with youth in fighting corruption. Civil society organisations in some MENA countries such as Tunisia have a track record in scrutinising government action and promoting integrity. Over the last few years, new civil society organisations were formed with an agenda to further transparency and open government. Professional associations of auditors and accountants have been spurred to expand activities and strengthen standards in their profession. Youth associations can play a similar role by evaluating the performance of public institutions with a youth portfolio in areas where the central government lacks the adequate capacities, especially at the local level.

Initiatives to engage youth in the fight against corruption are numerous around the world. Some are driven by governments, others by independent institutions, civil society and youth associations. In Hong Kong, the Independent Commission against Corruption (ICAC) developed online tools and applications tailored to young people's media use to promote integrity values (e.g. TV drama series, games, comics, social media presence). The work of ICAC (Box 5.1) provides a good example of using a youth lens to fighting corruption by raising early awareness among those who will take over responsibility in politics and the economy one day.

In the MENA region, civil society has taken advantage of the creativity of young people to increase resistance against the lure of corruption. Box 5.2 presents examples from Morocco and Tunisia that were successful in reconciling integrity messages with young people's general interests.

Box 5.1. **Tailor anti-corruption messages to youth through digital media: The example of the Independent Commission against Corruption (ICAC) in Hong Kong**

The Community Relations Department of the ICAC in Hong Kong makes use of digital media to inform youth about measures to foster integrity, transparency and fighting corruption.

ICAC hosts a website that shares the latest news of the Commission, and provides information on corruption prevention and access to audio-visual products and publications. The website "iTeenCamp" (www.iteencamp.icac.hk) teaches integrity values through online games, comics, quizzes, and interactive sections (e.g. polling, personality tests). The games are designed for different age groups. The TV drama series "ICAC Investigators" is targeting cineastes. ICAC is active on Facebook ("iTeen Xtra") and tweets about the detrimental effects of corruption.

Source: Independent Commission against Corruption of Hong Kong, www.iteencamp.icac.hk/EngIntro/Shows (accessed on 12 April 2016).

In the MENA region, civil society has taken advantage of the creativity of young people to increase resistance against the lure of corruption. Box 5.2 presents examples from Morocco and Tunisia that were successful in reconciling integrity messages with young people's general interests.

Box 5.2. **Fighting corruption on stage**

On International Anti-Corruption Day 2014, a variety of events – including music, dance and theatre happenings – gathered hundreds of youth on the streets of Casablanca to celebrate integrity and raise awareness about corruption. As part of a theatre piece, the youth-led project "*Paroles Urgentes*" distributed umbrellas to the crowd which formed a huge shield against the shower of corruption. In Tunisia, the civil society organisation I Watch hosted a poetry slam and stand-up comedy session to mobilise young people to vote in the parliamentary and presidential elections in 2014.

Source: Transparency International (2014b), "Anti-corruption kit: 15 ideas for young activists", http://issuu.com/transparencyinternational/docs/2014_anticorruptionkit_youth__en?e=2496456/8912943 (accessed on 10 April 2016).

Recommendations

MENA governments can engage with youth in strengthening integrity frameworks and fighting corruption in the public sector by:

1. **Involving youth in monitoring the implementation of policies, programmes and public services**, in particular at the local level, whether as volunteers or, preferably, contractors. This would provide governments with flexible support to monitoring and presents an opportunity for youth to acquire skills, potentially helping them to find more permanent positions, and participate in raising the

quality of services of immediate concern to them. Youth could also be tapped to help the government with analysis of existing data that is vital to the fight against corruption but has proven difficult to systematically tabulate and analyse. Where youth interest is high and confidentiality is not an issue, crowd-sourcing could also be used to expand data availability. Datasets with the potential to pull out and analyse youth- and gender-specific data would be especially appropriate for such uses.

2. **Promoting alliances to report abuse, misuse of resources and corruption** by building stronger partnerships between youth organisations, civil society organisations, independent institutions (e.g. anti-corruption agencies, ombudsman), and media.
3. **Establishing mechanisms and channels to encourage youth reporting of corruption**. Independent monitoring should be encouraged by providing for effective protection mechanisms. Current efforts of MENA countries to design legal frameworks for whistleblower protection (e.g. Tunisia), for instance, should ensure protection in areas where youth exposure to corruptive practices is particularly widespread.
4. **Strengthening communication efforts to raise awareness** among young people for existing standards of conduct in the public administration, citizen rights, and enforcement mechanisms. When interacting with public officials, youth should know about their rights to avoid abuse due to a lack of information.
5. **Support integrity awareness for students and other citizens**. Youth with skills in communications and those interested in teaching or training as a profession could be engaged on a temporary basis to develop and deliver training programmes for high school and college students and other audiences that could benefit from greater understanding of corruption and how to reduce it.

Public budgeting: Increase the impact of youth programming

The OECD "Recommendation of the Council on Budgetary Governance" characterises the public budget as the central policy document unfolding how government objectives will be prioritised and achieved. As such, it presents a powerful instrument of government policy to turn national plans and strategies into reality, and election pledges into tangible improvements. For a young person, the distributional impacts of policies as well as the share of public expenditures in critical public service areas (e.g. education, health) are hence of great interest.

The Recommendation addresses another angle of sound public financial management. It stresses the cross-fertilising role of good budgeting and modern public governance to achieve transparency, integrity, openness, participation, accountability, and ultimately build trust between public institutions and citizens.

Public budgets represent the key instrument for linking policy to objectives. Against the background of macroeconomic constraints and challenging economic prospects in key sectors (e.g. tourism), and overall low levels of investment and sluggish growth, an efficient use of public resources is more urgent than ever before. In this context, some MENA countries are currently undertaking ambitious reforms to link budgets to programmes, strategic priorities and objectives.

In Tunisia, the government introduced performance-based budgeting (*Gestion du Budget par Objectifs, GBO*) in 19 pilot ministries and is expected to adopt a new organic budget law by late 2016 or 2017 which will officially establish performance-based budgeting rules throughout the public administration. The reform aims at allocating public resources more efficiently and effectively with a view to improving the overall performance and control of public expenditures. In line with the recommendations provided by the OECD reports "Strengthening Fiscal Transparency for Better Public Governance in Tunisia" (2013a), "Towards better public governance : Performance-based budgeting" (forthcoming) and OECD support in publishing the country's Executive Budget in 2014 – a decision that allowed Tunisia to adhere to the OGP – the reform is expected to increase transparency and government performance.

Similar efforts have been undertaken in Morocco, which recently published the new Organic Finance Law (*Loi Organique relative à la loi de finances, LOLF*) in the Official Gazette. The LOLF aligns the management of public finances to the new arrangements as stipulated by the Constitution. Accordingly, following an initial phase with four pilot ministries, budgets will be designed around programmes. In the Palestinian Authority, despite progress in increasing budget transparency and accountability mechanisms, key challenges affect the introduction of result-based budgeting and medium-term fiscal expenditure frameworks. Jordan's first Action Plan submitted to the Open Government Partnership (2012-14) includes a commitment to assess the performance of government institutions against performance indicators and to upgrade the annual Government Units' Budgets Law in accordance with the advanced phases of result-oriented budgeting (ROB). The plan commits to enhancing the orientation towards programmes and activities related to "social, gender and child" along with resources allocated over the medium term (Open Government Partnership, n.d.).

Linking taxpayer's money to programmes and results rather than expenditure categories presents a potential leverage for aligning youth policy objectives with the allocation of public resources. In the definition of performance indicators and objectives, young people's interests need to be reflected. National development plans are the place for governments to define the broader strategies and objectives and how government policy is supposed to work towards these goals. Youth consultation in the elaboration of multi-annual development strategies is crucial and should not be left to the exclusive discretion of public officials.

If public budgets do not yet thrill young men and women, it is maybe because a sense for the critical importance it plays for the social and economic development of a country and the personal opportunities for the younger cohorts is largely absent. The Swedish International Development Cooperation Agency (SIDA) qualifies public financial management as "maybe the most powerful tool a government has to implement its policies and advance the rights of its population" and identifies seven reasons why children and youth should be integrated in a dialogue along the budget cycle (see Box 5.3).

Box 5.3. **Public financial management: The rights of children and young people**

1. **Public resources belong to the people of a country.** Available funds should be managed fairly and responsibly to serve the needs of the population.
2. **Children and young people are rights holders.** They are entitled to see their rights realised in practice. States are legally obliged to use their resources to realise these rights.
3. **It costs money to protect and advance the rights of children and young people.** The more efficiently and effectively resources are managed to meet human rights standards, the more services of better quality can be delivered to them.
4. **A country's budget reflects its real priorities in relation to development.** If a country is serious about prioritising the well-being of children and young people, this has to be reflected in its budget decisions and practices.
5. **Waste, mismanagement and corruption contribute to poor service delivery.** When services do not reach intended beneficiaries, it is particularly devastating for children and young people who are at risk or in danger, living with disabilities or in extreme poverty.
6. **What happens to today's children and young people will affect the country for decades to come.** A healthy, well-educated population is better prepared to meet tomorrow's challenges.
7. **The way a country raises revenue and the size of its debt burden has implications for future generations.** The children of today will face enormous challenges if they inherit state institutions and economies unable to provide for their people.

Source: Swedish International Development Cooperation Agency (2012), "Public financial management for the rights of children and young people", www.sida.se/contentassets/dfa19bd6efc84f25800edaa90590008e/public-financial-management-for-the-rights-of-children-and-young-people_3224.pdf (accessed on 1 April 2016).

A dialogue between public officials and youth about the allocation of public resources requires well-informed participants on both sides. For young people, an adequate presentation of budgetary information and data in a language that young people can understand is maybe the most important hurdle to clear in order to arouse young people's interest. For budgets to lose their scare factor, technical information should be translated into a visually appealing presentation, in particular in policy areas of immediate concern to young people. The mushrooming of citizens budgets in MENA countries, such as in Morocco (since 2012), Tunisia (since 2014), the Palestinian Authority (published in 2014) and Egypt (published for the first time in 2010 and again in 2014)[4] provides a good starting point to make budget information accessible for youth. The previous chapter on the role of digital technologies offers some pathways for governments to use the right channels for dissemination. Youth could be encouraged to participate in this process, for instance through a competition calling on young people to share their ideas for translating budget figures into policy messages and advice.

The government of Hong Kong presents budget data and information in a youth-friendly format (see Box 5.4).

Box 5.4. **Say it with a comic: How do public budgets affect youth affairs?**

For the 2010-11 budget, the government in Hong Kong produced a comic book to increase interest among youth to concern themselves with public budget and finance. It tells a story about young people facing several problems and how they learn about and try to influence the budget in order to address them. The comic book can be downloaded or may be read on line.

Additionally, the website provides a clear overview of "budget highlights" livened up by various cartoon characters. It introduces the strategic objectives of the government (consolidating recovery, economic development, caring society), and outlines a number of specific policies that are linked to the respective objective (e.g. Caring Society: Developing human capital supporting learning, promoting culture and sport, fighting drugs, strengthening public healthcare, caring for the needy, supporting jobseekers).

The website highlights examples of allocating public money to specific purposes (e.g. "provide a $1,000 allowance to students receiving student financial assistance. This will cost $570 million").

Source: Government of Hong Kong (2010), www.budget.gov.hk/2010/chi/flip/main.html (accessed on 12 April 2016).

The allocation of public resources is about making critical choices for the future of a society. Therefore, an inclusive approach to discuss the sources and beneficiaries of public funds is indispensable. All stakeholders, including youth, need the knowledge and capacity to engage with decision makers throughout the budget cycle, from planning to scrutinising public expenditures.

The city of Boston in the United States has shown confidence in, and openness towards, engaging young people in the allocation of public resources. Box 5.5 presents the "Youth Lead the Change" project that inspired other cities in the United States to organise participatory budgeting processes led by youth.

First experiences in involving young people in participatory budgeting processes have also been made in the MENA region. In Tunisia, citizens and in particular youth were invited to participate in the allocation of 2% of the municipal budget in La Marsa, Menzel Bourhuiba, Tozeur and Gabes in 2014. Most notably, in Menzel Bourguiba, the public authorities organised an awareness programme for citizens to encourage their participation in the relevant public meetings (Naser, 2014).

Box 5.5. **Youth Lead the Change: Youth-led participatory budgeting in Boston**

Boston has been a pioneer in organising youth-led participatory budgeting processes in the United States. In 2014, the city's "Youth Lead the Change" project for the first time gave teens and young adults (aged 12-25) an active role in deciding how USD 1 million of the city's budget should be invested. It is noteworthy that Boston's young people were engaged in all phases of the process including the design of projects, the discussion about spending priorities and the submission of the final project proposals. The latter were developed in joint meetings with city officials and city agencies.

Over one week, young Boston residents were able to vote for 4 out of 14 co-designed projects in four categories: education, community culture (e.g creating art spaces), parks/environment/health (e.g. renovating parks), and streets and safety. Voting sites in community centres, schools and T stops throughout the city collected the votes and, in many cases, brought young people for the first time to the ballot box.

Source: City of Boston, Department of Youth Engagement and Employment, http://youth.boston.gov/youth-lead-the-change/; Gilman, Hollie Russon (2014), "What happened when the City of Boston asked teenagers for help with the budget", 26 June, https://nextcity.org/daily/entry/boston-young-people-participatory-budgeting-winners-youth-lead-change (accessed on 12 April 2016).

The last example from Tunisia (Box 5.6) illustrates that youth can become involved in monitoring public expenditures and government performance to safeguard against the misuse and waste of public resources and corruption. Youth-led civil society organisations can partner with parliaments, control and audit bodies and independent institutions, such as ombudsman and anti-corruption agencies, in holding government to account. In particular, with the turn towards performance-based budgeting in MENA countries, performance audits could build on the expertise of young people to verify reported outcomes against reality on the ground.

Box 5.6. **Budget monitoring by youth-led civil society in Tunisia**

With the objective of monitoring government spending, the youth-led civil society organisation Al Bawsala initiated the project "Marsad Budget". The website aims at overcoming the technical character of public budgets and making them accessible and understandable for ordinary citizens to involve them in public debates about spending priorities and government performance.

The idea of Marsad Budget is to simplify budget data and information in order to facilitate the control of budget processes, and to inform the wider public about the design and implementation of regulatory initiatives. By drawing on data made available by the public administration and other sources, the website offers easy access, use, and comparison of budget and human resources data for the Parliament, the Presidency and the different ministries. It compiles information on the development of expenditures for each entity since 2012 and offers the possibility to download budget datasets and contact details. For the entities in which performance-based budgeting is operational, Marsad Budget outlines the allocation of resources along objectives.

Source: Al Bawsala (2016), "Marsad Budget", http://budget.marsad.tn/fr/ (accessed on 2 April 2016).

Recommendations

MENA governments can involve youth and hence foster a more inclusive approach to public budgeting by:

1. **Consulting youth organisations** and youth-led civil society organisations to identify meaningful programme indicators and objectives, especially in the context of the transition towards performance-based budgeting. An inclusive approach is likely to increase legitimacy and result in more ambitious and realistic targets.
2. **Publishing a citizen's budget that highlights youth-related expenditures** to illustrate the public investments made into the opportunities for young men and women (e.g. public spending in education, health, youth-specific projects and initiatives). Age-disaggregated data is likely to stimulate public debate about government performance and the priorities for youth-related expenditures.
3. **Involving youth in the allocation of public expenditures** through participatory budgeting approaches. The "Youth Lead the Change" project in Boston (see Box 5.5) illustrates that young men and women can participate in all stages of the budget process – from the submission of project ideas to the co-design of project proposals with local authorities and decision making by vote. Not least, youth-participatory budgeting presents an exercise in democratic decision making.
4. **Elaborating strategies to increase budget literacy among youth** to prepare them to critically reflect on public expenditures and hold government to account. Financial literacy presents a "core life skill" for youth to participate in modern society and choose between different career and education options and manage any discretionary funds they may have.[5]

Public human resource management: Remove structural obstacles to youth employment

As the region with the world's highest youth unemployment rate and the lowest female labour force participation, the MENA region is facing a number of structural obstacles that exclude large parts of society from contributing and benefiting from the economic development of their country.

High youth unemployment, in particular among young women, takes place in a context in which private sector development is weak and the public sector reached its limit to hire graduates from universities. Labour markets are characterised by insufficient capacity to absorb more qualified entrants and a prevalent mismatch of skills. This challenge is especially severe in countries like Morocco, Tunisia and Yemen in which 27-32% of enterprises report dissatisfaction with the competencies of young applicants. Dissatisfaction levels in the other countries covered in this report are considerably lower (6-12%) (World Bank, n.d.). Informal working arrangements often seem the only viable option to make a modest living, but often lack basic social or legal protection or employment benefits. In Egypt and the Palestinian Authority, around 51% and 57% of total employment is estimated to be informal, respectively.[6]

The mismatch between the supply and demand of youth labour

The rapid rise in tertiary education enrolments has encouraged youth to expect that they will find professional employment; many regard blue-collar work as unsuitable. Figure 5.1 compares the distribution of jobs held by employed youth in Egypt to the expectations of youth who still seek employment. Whereas 76% of jobseekers are looking for work as professionals or technicians, only 15% of the employed youth were able to find such work. Conversely, almost 60% of the employed youth hold jobs as craftsmen or other skilled blue-collar workers whereas less than 7% of unemployed youth would prefer this kind of work. The mismatch between the demand and the supply of labour points to structural deficiencies in many MENA economies and has resulted in growing dissatisfaction on the part of young graduates as well as employers.

Figure 5.1. **Occupations sought by Egyptian unemployed youth vs. those actually held by employed youth, 2014**

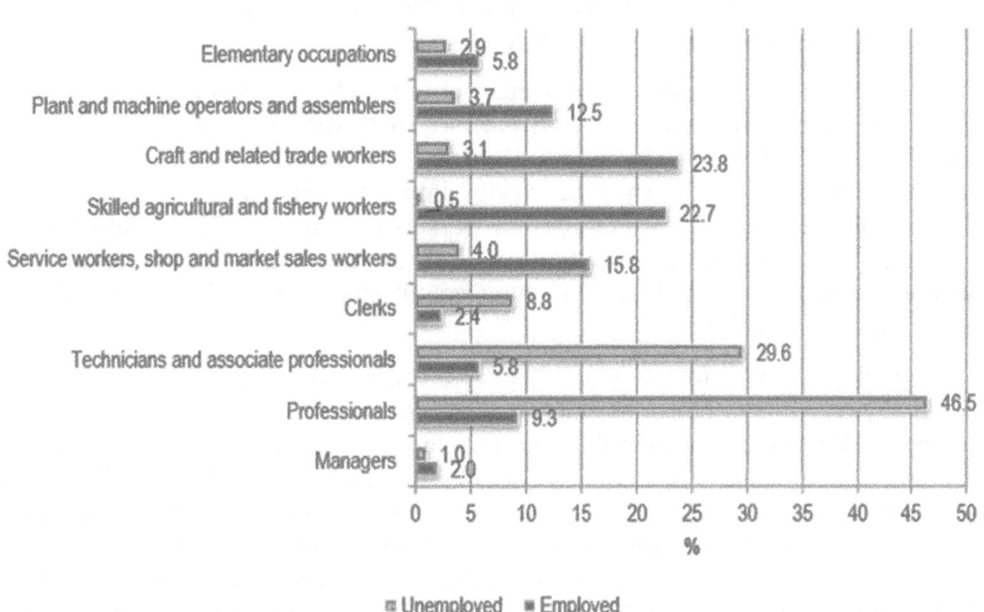

Source: Barsoum, Ghada, Mohamed Ramadan and Mona Mostafa (2014), "Labour market transitions of young women and men in Egypt", *Work4Youth Publication Series*, No. 16, June, ILO, Geneva.

There is no easy recipe to tackle the above-mentioned structural deficiencies. This section looks at the performance of public human resource management (HRM) systems, in line with the argument made by Afiouni, Ruël and Schuler (2014) and others that HRM management systems offer a potential pathway to foster youth's economic empowerment.

The preference for public sector employment despite increasing informality and the lack of HRM practices

OECD analysis of national HRM frameworks takes a multi-dimensional approach, including legal frameworks governing public employment, the composition of public employment, HR management (e.g. recruitment, compensation, performance management and workforce planning), public sector leadership and others. While a comprehensive analysis is outside the scope of this report, it will outline some of the key public HRM challenges MENA countries are facing today: a preference of young graduates for public sector work; an increase in informal employment within public institutions; and an absence of good HR practices in the public sector.

MENA governments remain under pressure to hire more youth. In the aftermath of the civil uprisings in some MENA countries, public sectors have experienced another surge of job creation mainly to appease popular demands and prevent already struggling economies from deteriorating further due to shrinking public demand. The National Employment and Self-Employment Agency (*Agence Nationale pour l'Emploi et le Travail Indépendant*) in Tunisia reports that 67 000 public sector jobs were created (OECD, 2015). As the OECD paper "Tackling youth unemployment in the MENA region" argues, this strategy has been exhausted and is no longer fiscally sustainable. And yet, public employment continues to be a major component in employment and a career objective for many young citizens especially women. The majority of these positions in the MENA region are service workers in education, health, and other government programmes such as public employment systems.

World Bank analysis of urban employment in Egypt, Jordan, Morocco, and Yemen reaffirms that a substantial share of youth is either employed in the public sector or in private-informal employment. In Egypt, Jordan, and Yemen, the share of urban employment in the public sector shows a broadly similar pattern, rising steadily from very low levels in the late teens to around 20% for workers reaching age 25 (Angel-Urdinola and Tanabe, 2012). In all four countries, however, the share of private-informal employment among youth aged 15-29 outnumbers all other forms of employment (e.g. public; private formal; self-employed).

The significant lack of formal jobs in the private sector is one of the key reasons for the popularity of public sector jobs among young graduates. On average, public sector employment offers higher salaries than the private sector, employment protection and special status, in particular with SOEs (O'Sullivan, Rey and Galvez Mendey, 2013). It is therefore no surprise that the MENA region used to have the highest central government wage bill in the world (as a percentage of gross domestic product) even when accounted for the fact that government employment in MENA is comparatively high (Ahmed et al., 2012). Given the popularity of public sector jobs, public sector queuing is a widespread phenomenon. In a recent OECD study over 65% of youth aged 15-29 in Tunisia indicate that they prefer to work in the government/public sector whereas only a minority of 22% favours the private sector and 10% self-employment (OECD, 2015). Data for youth in Egypt show similar results (Table 5.1).

Table 5.1. **Unemployed Egyptian youth by type of employer sought, gender, and area of residence, 2014**

In %

Employer sought	Total	Male	Female	Urban	Rural
Work for myself (own business/farm)	0.8	1.7	0.4	1.1	0.6
Work for the government/public sector	80.5	66.7	86.8	72.8	87.9
Work for a private company	17.4	30.3	11.6	23.6	11.5
Work for an international or organization	1.1	0.6	1.2	2.2	0.0
Work for family business/farm	0.2	0.6	0.0	0.4	0.0
Total	100.0	100.0	100.0	100.0	100.0

Source: Barsoum, Ghada, Mohamed Ramadan and Mona Mostafa (2014), "Labour market transitions of young women and men in Egypt", *Work4Youth Publication Series*, No. 16, June, ILO, Geneva.

Although the public sector is still the first choice of MENA graduates, informality *within* the public sector is increasing. World Bank data indicates that the share of informal employment within the public sector amounts to 11% in Egypt, 12% in Yemen, 18% in Morocco, and 31% in Jordan (Angel-Urdinola and Tanabe, 2012). While no age-disaggregated data exists, the overall pattern of informality suggests that the willingness to accept short-term contracts in the absence of permanent positions is higher among youth. In Egypt, teachers may even be hired on daily contracts. These workers may hope that a short-term contract will give them better access to permanent employment, but this is uncertain at best. Informally employed youth suffer from the lack of social protection, labour legislation and protective measures in the workplace and are more likely to become subject to abusive work practices (Wally, 2012).

Another challenge for young graduates is the absence of good practices in HR management in the public sector. Workforce planning is currently very limited in MENA countries. This leaves recruitment and compensation decisions to the discretion of individuals instead of being responsive to labour market developments and performance criteria. Figure 5.2 illustrates that personal relationships rather than public employment services play the main role in placing youth into public sector (and private sector) jobs in Egypt and Tunisia.

Figure 5.2. **Sources of job search assistance reported by youth who found jobs, Egypt and Tunisia, 2014**

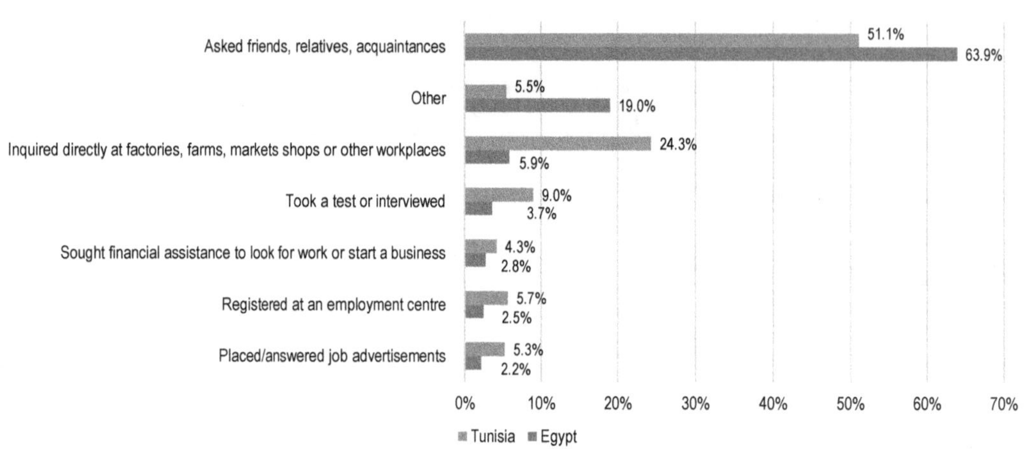

Note: Some categories are combined for clarity and consistency.

Source: Barsoum, Ghada, Mohamed Ramadan and Mona Mostafa (2014), "Labour market transitions of young women and men in Egypt", *Work4Youth Publication Series*, No. 16, June, ILO, Geneva;.Observatoire National de l'Emploi et des Qualifications (2014), "Transition vers le marché du travail des jeunes femmes et hommes en Tunisie", *Work4Youth Publication Series*, No. 15, June, ILO, Geneva.

The introduction of merit-based and more standardised recruitment processes could especially encourage young women to apply for senior positions who may find it more difficult to move up the ladder in an environment in which leadership positions are dominated by men and awarded through connections (OECD/CAWTAR, 2014).

Recommendations

MENA governments can foster the long-term employment opportunities for youth in the public sector by:

1. **Reinforcing standardised and merit-based recruitment and promotion** to recruit young graduates with the necessary skills and competencies, and encourage women to apply for senior level positions in the public sector.

2. **Monitoring such practices as contract-based hiring in the public sector** to avoid abuse. Experience demonstrates that short-term contracts offer flexibility in meeting variable personnel needs, but also opens up undesirable avenues for abusive HR practices, such as denial of benefits, which can affect youth with little professional experience disproportionally.

3. **Introducing placement systems into schools**, beginning with middle school, to support students who are entering the job market. Second-chance systems are also needed for young workers to enable them to continue their education on a more flexible basis.

4. **Revitalising staff development and training programmes in the public sector**. This would help the countries of the MENA region to prepare for the turnover in mid-level and higher ranks, preparing younger managers to move into place as older workers retire. Many of these programmes have been under-resourced for years and would benefit greatly from increased analytic and policy content in

curricula, linking training more closely to job responsibilities, and engaging the private sector.

5. **Introducing better human resource planning and management** to enable governments to identify upcoming needs for skills where youth have an advantage, such as ICTs management, and to expand leadership development programmes that cultivate young managers with leadership potential.

Regulatory policy: Increase regulatory quality for inclusive policy making and job creation

Mainstreaming a youth perspective in regulatory policy

The 2012 OECD "Recommendation of the Council on Regulatory Policy and Governance" defines regulatory policy as the "process by which government, when identifying a policy objective, decides whether to use regulation as a policy instrument, and proceeds to draft and adopt a regulation through evidence-based decision making" (OECD, 2012). Regulatory policy is embedded in a broader framework comprising the government's core policies, systems, processes and tools, and actors, institutions and capacities (OECD, 2013b).

By adhering to the Open Government Partnership, Jordan and Tunisia committed to pursue regulatory policy with a view to reinforcing openness, transparency, citizen participation and accountability. The Palestinian Authority has identified OGP membership as a strategic objective and lever to build state institutions. Morocco is working towards fulfilling the eligibility criteria. Recently, both OECD and MENA countries discovered the potential of OGP Action Plans to further the cause of young people. For instance, Finland's Open Government Action Plan 2015-2017 identifies the increased participation of children and youth as a horizontal theme and lays out concrete commitments to improve the possibilities of children and youth to influence the decisions that concern them, for instance by providing advice to the staff of state government and the municipalities on how to engage different age groups (Open Government Partnership, 2015).

Assessing the impact of regulation on youth

Any regulation implies costs and benefits that can be shared by different segments of society to quite different extents. By assessing the impact of new and existing legislation on vulnerable groups in society, such as youth, governments can anticipate the distributional effects of regulatory policy and, if necessary, make adjustments. Through the integration of a youth perspective into *ex ante* impact assessments (e.g. regulator impact assessments, RIA) and *ex post* evaluations, governments can assess the welfare effects for youth in order to avoid creating additional burden for this age group. However, the 2013 OECD Review, *Regulatory Reform in the Middle East and North Africa*, which assesses the regulatory environment in MENA countries against the 2009 Regional Charter for Regulatory Quality and the 2012 OECD Recommendation of the Council on Regulatory Policy and Governance, found that RIAs are not yet systematically used in MENA countries.

The Better Regulation Toolbox developed by the European Commission presents three core questions to guide policy makers in assessing the impact of new regulation on youth (Box 5.7).

Box 5.7. Better Regulation Toolbox by the European Commission

The Tool Box is structured around 8 main chapters and includes 59 tools. Tool 26provides a set of questions for policy makers to assess the impact of new regulations on youth.

- **Is there an impact on social inclusion and integration of youth?** Provided that youth present a group particularly prone to certain measures, and can often face risk of exclusion and insufficient socio-economic integration, analysis of how these can affect this group is necessary to avoid possible negative outcomes. Well-being and the ability to participate in democratic life, including in cross-border programmes and activities, should also be taken into account.
- **Is there an impact on learning opportunities in respect to youth?** Identifying these is important due to the fact that youth is a vital part of educational activities, while education plays a key role in development of this group. Potential impacts on youth in terms of learning opportunities can be thus analysed by reviewing the section on education impacts with respect to youth.
- **Is there an impact on labour market, continuity of transition between education and professional performance in respect to youth?** Aspects such as effects on activation of young people in terms of employment and self-employment, period between leaving education and finding a first job, transition from internships to work contract, as well as potential impacts on population of young people out of employment, education and training should be considered in this part.

Source: European Commission (2015), "Better Regulation Toolbox", http://ec.europa.eu/smart-regulation/guidelines/docs/br_toolbox_en.pdf (accessed on 12 April 2016).

Regulatory policy sets the legal framework in which citizens and businesses operate. Sound regulatory frameworks create legal certainty for private companies to do business whereas heavy administrative burden discourages economic activity among potential young entrepreneurs and job creation for young graduates. With a view to the existing regulatory framework, the *Ease of Doing Business Index* by the World Bank compares how easy it is for domestic firms to start and operate a business. Table 5.2 compares the performance of the MENA countries which are examined in this report.

Table 5.2. **Measuring business regulations: Ease of doing business in selected MENA countries, 2014**

Country	Rank	Top 50	Lowest 50
Tunisia	60	Getting electricity, trading across borders	-
Morocco	71	Trading across borders	-
Egypt	112	-	Dealing with construction permits, paying taxes, enforcing contracts
Jordan	117	Getting electricity, paying taxes	Getting credit, protecting minority investors, resolving insolvency
Yemen	137	Registering property	Starting a business, getting credit, protecting minority investors, resolving insolvency
Palestinian Authority	143	-	Starting a business, dealing with construction permits, protecting minority investors, resolving insolvency
Libya	188	-	Starting a business, dealing with construction permits, registering property, getting credit, protecting minority investors, paying taxes, trading across borders, resolving insolvency

Note: Countries are ranked on their ease of doing business, from 1–189. A high ease of doing business ranking means the regulatory environment is more conducive to the starting and operation of a domestic firm. The index includes a total of ten categories. The top/lowest 50 categories were added by the author to highlight categories in which the selected MENA countries figure among the best (1-50) or lowest (139-189) ranked countries.

Source: World Bank (2014), *Economy Rankings database*, Doing Business - Measuring Business Regulations, www.doingbusiness.org/rankings.

Recent research provides evidence that removing regulatory barriers is associated with increased job creation. Analysis of sustained periods of broad job creation found that they were strongly associated with good governance. Rapid, deep and sustained falls in unemployment resulted when government effectiveness increased, along with control of corruption, rule of law, and political stability, and where regulatory quality improved, as shown by a drop in the time required to enforce contracts, to complete import and export transactions, and to start a business (Freund and Rijkers, 2012).

Recommendations

With the adoption of the 2009 Regional Charter for Regulatory Quality and in accordance with the 2012 OECD "Recommendation of the Council on Regulatory Policy and Governance" MENA countries could move towards a more inclusive and youth-sensitive approach to regulatory policy by:

1. **Mainstreaming open and inclusive government principles across the whole of government** with a view to engaging youth more systematically in policy making and public consultations. In line with the recent practice of some OECD countries, member countries to the OGP can foster youth engagement through concrete commitments in their Action Plan – a document that benefits from the input of public officials and civil society (e.g. youth associations) alike.

2. **Gradually introducing regulatory impact assessments and cost-benefit-analysis**. Despite the fact that RIAs are currently not used systematically in MENA countries, new regulation with considerable distributional effects should be examined to anticipate the share of costs and benefits among different

segments of society, including youth and relevant sub-groups (e.g. male/female, urban/rural).

3. **Reviewing the stock of existing legislation** in order to consign redundant and inefficient provisions to history books, lighten the administrative burden and create an economic environment that encourages business activity, youth entrepreneurship and job creation.

Local governance: Promote youth engagement at all levels of government

The local level is the place where youth interact most regularly with public authorities and institutions use public services and participate in the development of their society as volunteers. The discontent with public service delivery at the local level was one of the factors that provoked mass protests among the young generation in some MENA cities in 2011. Representing the closest public authority to supply and deliver basic services, the protests targeted the municipalities before turning into demonstrations that reached the capital cities. The specific social and economic context and challenges faced by youth in big cities, metropolitan areas, or rural areas calls for tailored approaches to counteract political apathy or frustration, in particular among youth living in disadvantaged regions.

Decentralisation as an opportunity to promote youth engagement and deliver tailored youth policy

The MENA countries examined in this report are characterised by a long tradition of centralised systems in which the capital city has exercised great discretionary power over collecting and managing public resources. This has excluded many remote areas and their population from an equal access to government assistance and access to critical services. In the past, youth policies were formulated in the capital cities without the systematic involvement of public officials and civil society from the sub-national level. In recent years, however, a call for more decentralised governance frameworks has been sweeping through some of the studied MENA countries. The gradual transfer of competencies to public authorities at the sub-national level has the potential to redefine the way youth policy is being design and implemented. For instance, Egypt's new constitution calls for greater autonomy for local administrations, which are at present only branches of the national government. The 2014 Constitution of Tunisia stipulates that local communities have their own legal personality and financial and administrative autonomy, and hence manage local affairs in conformity with the principles of free administration. An explicit reference to a decentralised organisation of the state is also made in the Moroccan Constitution of 2011. In Jordan, the parameters for decentralisation reform are defined in the Municipality Law and the Decentralisation Law which were approved by the Parliament in 2015.

For the time being, however, central governments still assume wide discretionary power at the sub-national level through their line ministries. Local authorities suffer from weak institutional capacities to shape programmes and heavily depend on transfers and subsidies due to a lack of fiscal autonomy (Bergh, 2014). In countries in which decentralisation has progressed, many important services for youth remain under national control and administration. Local schools, for example, still report to national ministries of education, although some countries, such as Egypt, have introduced local advisory boards, enabling parents and local employers to have a modicum of influence on schooling. They do not have the capacity to influence curriculum, however, and, are not autonomous. It yet remains to be seen if the current decentralisation efforts will indeed result in more inclusive policy making and greater discretionary power among local actors to identify and implement policy priorities.

In a decentralised environment, local stakeholders across the territory must be able to participate in the identification of policy priorities to inform national youth policies and development strategies. In turn, for an effective implementation of youth programmes on the ground, local authorities and institutions must be able to rely on adequate human, technical and financial capacities. The mutual dependence of the different levels of government in the design and delivery of youth policy points to the importance of effective vertical co-ordination mechanisms, such as in the form of opportunities for deliberation among public officials and youth representatives from all levels.

Engaging youth in a context of rapid urbanisation and neglected remote areas

Rapid urbanisation has been a common trend in most of the studied MENA countries. In Jordan, the share of the urban population is higher than in the average of OECD countries. In Egypt and Yemen, the share of the urban populations considerably lower, however, in both countries the urban population heavily concentrates in the biggest city. As of 2014, Cairo accounts for more than half the overall urban population in Egypt; Sanaa hosts around one-third of all urban Yemenis (see Figure 5.3).

Figure 5.3. **Share of urban population and population in the largest city, as percentage of urban population in selected MENA countries, and OECD average, 2014**

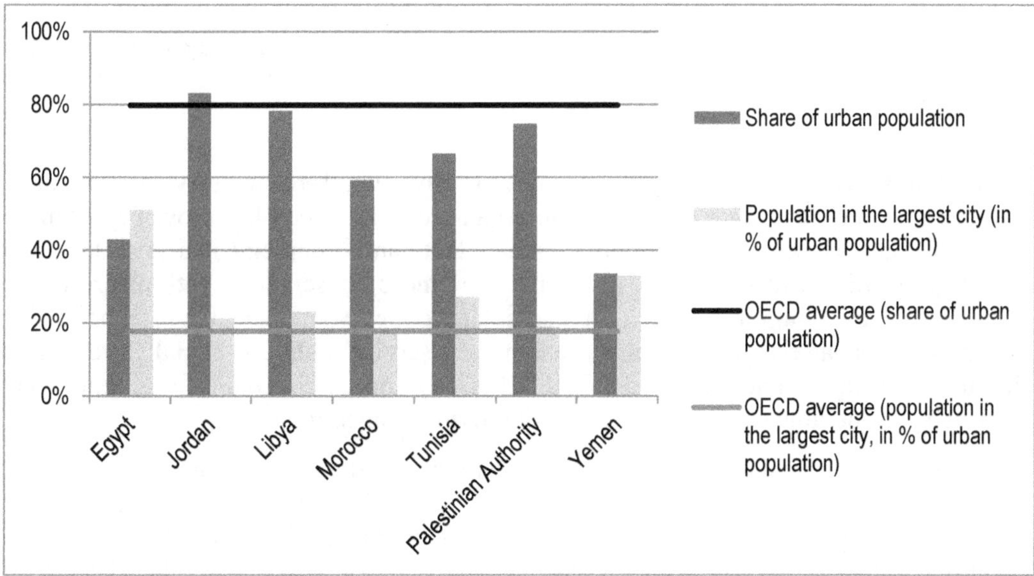

Note: OECD data presents the unweighted average.

Source: OECD's own work based on World Bank (n.d.a), "Urban population (% of total)", http://data.worldbank.org/indicator/SP.URB.TOTL.IN.ZS; "Population in the largest city (% of urban population)", http://data.worldbank.org/indicator/EN.URB.LCTY.UR.ZS/countries, United Nations, World Urbanization Prospects (accessed on 10 April 2016). and .

The popularity of cities and metropolitan areas is placing a heavy burden on national policy makers and city managers to address recurrent traffic jams, environmental degradation, and a lack of adequate housing, education and jobs. Figure 5.4 shows that only 3.5 million people lived in MENA cities, with a population of more than 1 million in 1950, compared to almost 80 million today. This figure is projected to rise to nearly 100 million within ten years.

Figure 5.4. **Combined population in Arab cities with 1+ million people, 1950-2025**

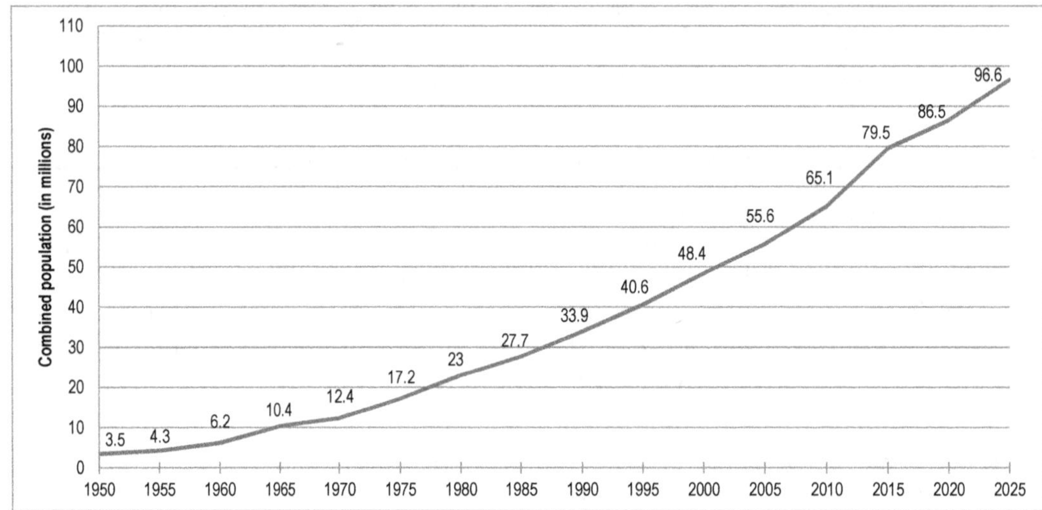

Source: UN Habitat (2012), *The State of Arab Cities 2012 - Challenges of Urban Transition,* Regional Cities Reports, http://unhabitat.org/books/the-state-of-arab-cities-2012-challenges-of-urban-transition/ (accessed on 2 April 2016).

In rural areas, institutional state capacities to deliver youth-related services are scarce. Although poverty levels are higher than in urban areas, this need has proven resistant to translation into successful programming models that can be implemented at scale. Rural societies in MENA, as elsewhere, also tend to be more conservative with regard to the roles played by youth in society, in particular young women, and hence offer few channels to engage them in policy making or service delivery. Finally, territorial disparities are a common concern of all MENA countries covered in this report and present a considerable obstacle for youth from disadvantaged regions.

Youth are particularly exposed to the current shortcomings, but few formal or informal channels exist through which they can voice their ideas. There is a more general lack of participatory mechanisms at the sub-national level, which leaves weakly organised actors in society with no say in local decision making. In the absence of inclusive institutions and procedures, exclusive institutions tend to strengthen the voice of the already dominant groups in society. With a gradual increase of competencies in local institutions in some of the study countries, there is a momentum for institutional reform and opening up ways for a more structured and systematic engagement of youth.

OECD member countries have embarked on this process for some years, although to differing degrees. Finland ranks among the most progressive countries in this regard. Since 2006, according to Finland's Youth Act, "the opportunity to participate in the handling of issues relating to local and regional youth work and policy must be provided for young people. Additionally, young people must be heard during the handling of issues concerning them" (Schauer and Klinzing, 2012). Making youth participation mandatory by law reflects advice provided by the Council of Europe which argues that the "active participation of young people in decisions and actions at local and regional level is essential if we are to build more democratic, inclusive and prosperous societies" (Council of Europe, 2013).

Strategies for youth engagement at the local level

Youth engagement at the local level can take many different forms. The concrete space given to youth to express their interests vis-à-vis local authorities will depend on the maturity of local governance frameworks as well as the organisational structure in each country. To start with, MENA government could open up public hearings and consultation meetings and provide incentives for young people to participate. Initiatives aimed at bringing young people together with local representatives, such as by the Tunisian civil society organisation I Watch, must be scaled up and become institutionalised to avoid giving the impression of mere decorative events. I Watch organised roundtable discussions in different municipalities, gathering young people and local representatives to raise awareness of mechanisms for youth to participate in local decision making and get involved in municipal elections. A promising government-led approach in this area has been launched by the National Observatory of Youth at the Ministry of Youth and Sports in Tunisia, called "*Agora – Débat de la ville*" (Box 5.8).

Box 5.8. **Strengthening the foundations for dialogue between youth and local authorities**

The *Agora – Débat de la ville* project in Tunisia aims at strengthening the free expression of youth in a context in which communication spaces and a permanent dialogue between youth and local authorities is absent.

The project's target group are young people from the periphery of cities, members of youth organisations and youth centres. It co-operates with various societal actors, in particular youth and sports facilities, municipal youth centres, the Arab Centre for Media Training and Studies and the British Council.

Noting that few if any public spaces exist for youth to discuss politics and the future of their neighbourhoods with local authorities, the project focuses on three priority areas:

- **The creation of web community radios**: To create a space for relevant information for youth and debate between youth and local authorities.
- **The training of 150 youth leaders that are active in their communities**: To train other youth in terms of communication, participation in public life, active citizenship and local democracy.
- **The organisation of city debates**: To introduce dialogue between youth of specific districts, and between youth and public authorities within youth centres.

Source: *Observatoire National de la Jeunesse* (2016), "Projet AGORA débat de la ville", www.onj.nat.tn/index.php/fr/projets/projet-agora-debat-de-la-ville (accessed on 1 April 2016).

The project presents an encouraging example for strengthening youth's voice and capacities to interact with local authorities on a more regular basis. A possible alternative pathway could be to allow for young people's direct consultation in local and regional councils or the creation of local youth councils. Media and civil society organisations both have a critical role to play by opening up spaces for dialogue and consolidating young people's voices for a more powerful message *vis-à-vis* local authorities.

In Morocco, the new Constitution of 2011 requires policy makers to take into account the concerns of young people in the design of development plans and programme delivery in local municipalities (see Chapter 3). Reportedly, local youth councils have been established with the support of international donors in cities such as El Jadida, Assilah, Salé and Fes but from a nationwide perspective, they leave much of the territory uncovered (Rabbaa, 2015). For these councils to facilitate dialogue between youth and local authorities, a legal framework needs to be established to define their duties and responsibilities as well as the mechanisms for dialogue.

Good practices to engage youth at local level

The benefits of strengthening the voice of youth in local policy making and public service delivery are fairly obvious. First, youth are heavy users of public services that emerge as issues of local concern, such as basic infrastructure services (e.g. water and sanitation, waste collection and management, transport, energy), social services (education, health, housing, elderly and childcare) and quality-of-life services (e.g. public safety, urban planning, culture and entertainment, sport, public space) (United Cities and Local Governments, 2013). In the absence of youth or a serious broker representing their concerns, scarce resources may end up being spent elsewhere. Second, youth can engage more easily than is generally possible in large, complex national bureaucracies. In line with the arguments put forward in Chapter 4, youth involvement in local consultations and participatory processes provides venues in which young men and women can develop their understanding of government processes, train advocacy skills, and expand their network of relationships. A more systematic involvement can increase the legitimacy of the overall decision-making process and make an important contribution to building trust between policy makers and younger citizens.

It is important to note, however, that an elite-led project limited to highly educated youth risks creating new divides. For instance, given that young women face additional barriers to participation, possible obstacles to their involvement need to be removed (see Chapter 2) (Refstie, 2012). Finland's Initiative Channel, an online tool to broaden the participation base in community affairs, was successful to reach out to youth. The Initiative Channel is presented in Box 5.9.

Box 5.9. Local communities give youth a voice on line: Finland's Initiative Channel

Through the Initiative Channel, Finnish communities have given young people an opportunity to make their voices heard on line and contribute to the development of their neighbourhoods. Young people could post their ideas, before they were being put to a vote. The most promising ideas had the chance to be turned into real initiatives in partnership with local authorities.

The e-democracy service corresponds to the strategic goals of Finland's Child and Youth Policy Development Programme 2012-15 and Section 8 of Finland's Youth Act, which makes youth participation mandatory.

By August 2015, the website reported around 245 000 visitors and almost 15 000 comments. Recently, the website was replaced by a new service entitled nuortenideat ("young people's ideas").

Source: Nuortenideat (2016), https://www.nuortenideat.fi/fi/ ; Koordinatti Development Centre of Youth Information and Counselling (n.d.), www.koordinaatti.fi/sites/default/files/koordinaatti-and-initiative-channel.pdf (accessed on 10 April 2016).

Box 5.10. European Youth Capital

The European Youth Capital (EYC) is a title awarded by the European Youth Forum, a platform representing 99 national youth councils and international youth organisations.

The European Youth Capital is given the chance to showcase, through a multi-faceted programme, the opportunities for its young population to participate in cultural, social, political and economic life and development.

During an EYC year, the host city holds events and projects designed to demonstrate the active, essential role that young people and youth organisations can and do play in society; and thus lead to significant change in terms of sustainable long-term youth participation in the city.

Source: European Youth Capital (2016), www.europeanyouthcapital.org/about/ (accessed on 12 April 2016).

Recommendations

MENA governments could promote inclusive youth engagement across the different levels of government by:

1. **Providing effective and permanent channels** for youth from all socio-economic backgrounds to contribute to the identification of local youth needs and hold local authorities accountable, such as through local youth councils. These councils should be given real influence in the decision-making process to avoid creating the impression of mere decorative events.
2. **Implementing communication channels**, such as community-based and youth-led radios, that offer a space for young people to interact with local authorities, seek information on local affairs and inform their friends and fellow youth of opportunities to engage.

3. **Involving young people at the different sub-national levels to participate in the identification of public service needs and their implementation and monitoring**, such as by providing incentives to volunteer and contribute to the development of their neighbourhood.

4. **Engaging with local universities and technical institutes**, which are a natural channel to engage youth productively and help them build job-relevant skills as well as making connections with potential future employers.

Gender equality: Tackling the structural and cultural barriers to equal opportunities

Young women in the MENA region confront gender-based barriers and obstacles associated with their status as youth. The situation for young women is therefore often described as a double challenge that affects all dimensions of participation, namely in politics, society and the economy. For instance, the employment gap among young men and women exceeds those in all other regions of the world, as shown in Figure 5.5. If the economic participation of women in MENA countries is low, it is even more difficult for young women to find decent jobs. As Figure 5.6 shows, this gap is particularly significant in Egypt, Libya and the Palestinian Authority, where more than half to two-thirds of young females are unemployed compared to 25-40% of total female unemployment. In Morocco and Tunisia, this gap is considerably smaller, but still striking.

These findings come at a time when progress has been made towards achieving gender equality in education. Today, the gap between male and female literacy is much smaller among youth than among older population segments; and the proportion of women compared to men in tertiary education has moved beyond parity in some countries, such as the Palestinian Authority. However, obstacles in the legal frameworks, institutions and policies as well as prevailing traditional views on women's roles in society disadvantage young women to move from education into jobs.

The OECD report, *Women in Public Life: Gender, Law and Policy in the Middle East and North Africa* (hereafter, "2014 MENA Gender Report"), finds that the employment gap is only one among several divides that prevent women from participating in economic, social and public life in the same fashion men do (OECD/CAWTAR, 2014).

Figure 5.5. **Youth unemployment by region and gender, 2004-12**

Average (%)

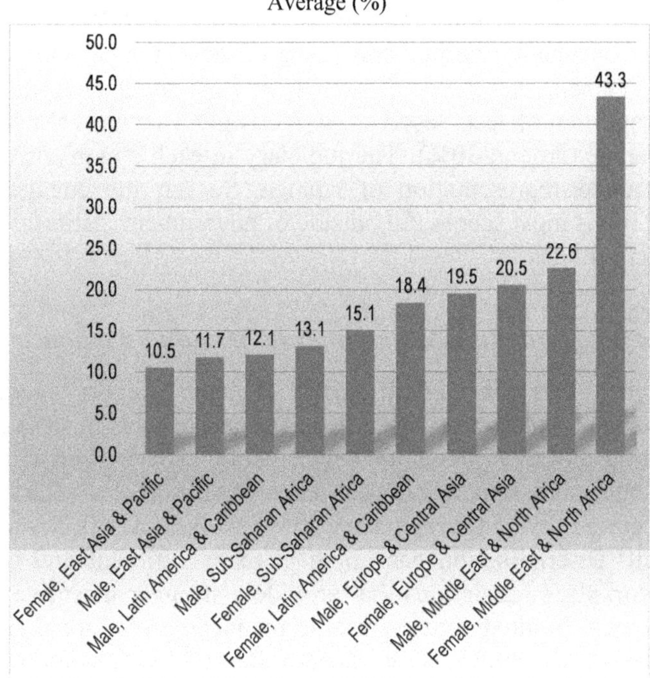

Source: Modeled ILO estimate, WDI data.

Figure 5.6. **Male and female unemployment rates in selected MENA countries, total working age population and youth, 2014 (or latest available year)**

%

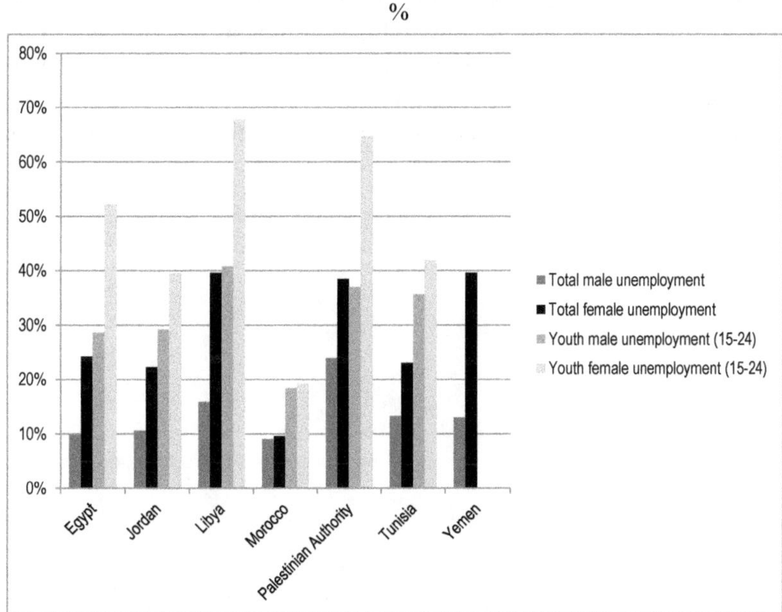

Note: Latest available data for each country. Tunisia (total: 2013, youth: 2012); Morocco (total: 2013, youth: 2012); Jordan (all 2013); Egypt (all 2013), Yemen (2004); Palestinian Authority (total: 2014, youth: 2013), Libya (all 2012). The Palestinian Authority is referred to in the ILO statistics as West Bank and Gaza Strip. For Jordan, disaggregated data is available for age groups 15-19 (male: 34.4%, female: 22.8%) and 20-24 (male: 24.1%, female: 56.2%). Data shown presents the unweighted average. No youth data is available for Yemen.

Source: OECD's own work based on World Bank (n.d.) "Unemployment, female (% of female labor force)"; "Unemployment, male (% of male labor force)"; "Unemployment, youth female (% of female labor force ages 15-24)"; "Unemployment, youth male (% of male labor force ages 15-24)" (all modeled ILO estimate), http://data.worldbank.org/indicator/.

Although women enjoy equal rights as men to participate in political life according to the Constitution of Morocco, the Palestinian Authority and Yemen, overall women's representation in consultative bodies and parliaments in the selected MENA countries remains low. In Yemen, the share of women in parliament does not exceed the 1% granted by the proportion of seats reserved. In fact, only Tunisia is reaching levels similar to the OECD average (around 30%). The judiciary in each country is also characterised by a significant under-representation of women. So far, the engagement of (young) women in public life is most successful outside of government institutions, for instance in civil society organisations.

Obstacles to the economic self-determination of young women

OECD evidence from the 2014 MENA Gender Report suggests that public governance frameworks and traditional roles assigned to women in society both play a role in perpetuating an environment in which young women find it particularly more difficult to enjoy the same opportunities as men. Despite recent efforts to remove legal discriminations in the existing regulatory frameworks of MENA countries, biased provisions prevail. Discrimination can come in many different and oftentimes hidden forms, such as workplace regulations that provide a stronger incentive for employers to hire men over women. Limited opportunities to reconcile professional and family life and uneven salary checks for the same job – prevailing practices in most OECD countries too – can place an additional burden on women.

Table 5.3 explores some of the workplace regulations which can negatively affect (young) women. The table demonstrates the importance of analysing the conditions in each country at sector-level. It points to the fact that provisions with a seemingly positive connotation (e.g. restricted access to jobs which are considered to be too hazardous or arduous) may actually put the brakes on women's participation in the labour force. These challenges cannot be overcome if they are addressed at the sector-level but require a more general commitment to establish equal opportunities for young men and women.

Table 5.3. **Do women have equal rights in the workplace in MENA countries?**

Working hours and industry restrictions	Egypt	Jordan	Morocco	Palestinian Authority	Tunisia	Yemen	Percent "No"
Can non-pregnant and non-nursing women do the same jobs as men?	No	No	No	No	No	No	100%
Can non-pregnant and non-nursing women engage in the following occupations in the same way as men?							
Mining	No	No	No	No	No	Yes	83%
Construction	No	No	Yes	Yes	Yes	Yes	33%
Metalwork	No	No	Yes	No	No	Yes	67%
Factory work	No	No	Yes	Yes	Yes	Yes	33%
Jobs requiring lifting weights above a certain amount	No	No	Yes	Yes	Yes	Yes	33%
Jobs deemed hazardous	No	Yes	No	No	Yes	No	67%
Jobs deemed arduous	No	Yes	No	No	Yes	No	67%
Jobs deemed morally inappropriate	No	Yes	Yes	Yes	Yes	No	33%
Can non-pregnant and non-nursing women work the same night hours as men?	No	No	No	No	No	No	100%
Does the law mandate equal remuneration for men and women for work of equal value?	No	No	Yes	No	No	No	83%
Are there laws mandating non-discrimination based on gender in hiring?	No	No	Yes	No	No	No	83%
Is it illegal for an employer to ask about family status during a job interview?	No	No	No	No	No	No	100%
Are there laws penalizing or preventing the dismissal of pregnant women?	Yes	Yes	Yes	Yes	Yes	No	17%
Must employers give employees an equivalent position when they return from maternity leave?	No	Yes	Yes	No	No	No	67%
Are employers required to provide break time for nursing mothers?	Yes	Yes	Yes	Yes	Yes	Yes	0%
Do employees with minor children have rights to a flexible/part time schedule?	No	No	No	No	No	No	100%
Percent "No"	88%	65%	41%	65%	53%	65%	63%

Source: World Bank (2013), *Women, Business and the Law 2014: Removing Restrictions to Enhance Gender Equality*,. World Bank, Washington DC, http://wbl.worldbank.org/~/media/WBG/WBL/Documents/Reports/2014/Women-Business-and-the-Law-2014-Key-Findings.pdf?la=en (accessed on 1 April 2016).

Traditional gender roles discourage the economic activity of young women in many MENA countries. Work-life balance measures such specific entitlements for pregnant women or flexible start and working hours contribute to create an environment that encourages young women to enter the labour market. Table 5.4 illustrates to what degree the countries examined in this report, Lebanon, and selected Gulf countries have introduced suchlike measures to increase flexibility in professional life. It illustrates that while some of the most basic requirements as set out by the International Labour

Organization are met, other benefits are very unevenly offered. Although personal and family relationships may provide an alternative to legal entitlements, the absence of effective measures for women to participate in economic life is likely to perpetuate and enforce traditional gender roles.

Table 5.4. **Work-life balance measures in selected MENA countries for employees of the central civil service, 2014**

	Yemen	Egypt	Lebanon	Jordan	Tunisia	Morocco	Bahrain	Palestinian Authority	Kuwait	United Arab Emirates
Specific measures for breastfeeding women	x	x		x	x	x	x	x	x	x
Leave for sick family member		x		x		x	x		x	x
Specific measures for pregnant women	x	x		x			x		x	x
Leave for elderly family member		x		x	x		x			x
Part-time employment solutions	x	x			x		x			x
Flexible start and working hours and time saving	x	x					x			x
Employer provided childcare facilities		x		x						x
Subsidies for childcare		x				x				x
Condensed/compressed work week							x			x
Teleworking										x
Other	x				x		x			x
Total	5	8	-	5	4	3	8	1	3	11

Source: OECD/CAWTAR (2014), *Women in Public Life: Gender, Law and Policy in the Middle East and North Africa*, OECD Publishing, Paris, http://dx.doi.org/10.1787/9789264224636-en.

Finally, initiatives aimed at strengthening partnerships between business, government and academia should be gender-sensitive to allow female graduates a smoother transition from university to workplace. The paper of the MENA-OECD Competitiveness Programme suggests that women seeking jobs or career guidance should benefit from tailored services just like young female entrepreneurship to offer alternative pathways to economic self-determination.

Obstacles to the engagement of young women in public life

Women in the selected MENA countries are facing significant barriers to raise their voice in the political discourse. Although some civil society institutions feature the participation of young and very engaged young women, these positive examples cannot reverse a general trend that women are significantly under-represented in both official positions and public life more generally. Similar to patterns in OECD countries, the 2014 MENA Gender Report finds that the disparities between men and women increase as one climbs the organisational ladder. The gap in the top management of the civil service, for instance, varies between 9% in Tunisia and 78% in the Palestinian Authority in favour of men. This gap is even larger in the judicial sector. Whereas women are already significantly underrepresented in the Supreme Court in OECD countries (28%), available data for the selected MENA countries suggests that only 2 out of 48 judges of the constitutional court are women (4%) (World Bank, n.d.).[7]

Even if participation in executive bodies plays less of a role for young women who still lack work experience to carry out such duties, the absence of women in leadership positions shapes the overall perception of women's role as there are few role models to look up to. Evidence from Tunisia suggests that young women in the MENA region are also more likely to abstain from voting and engaging in political parties (National Democratic Institute, 2012). Moreover, Figure 5.7 shows that women are less likely to be engaged in civic activities than their male counterparts. MENA governments need to tackle this phenomenon decisively as the absence of women as active citizens risks reinforcing programmes and institutional frameworks that fail to deliver on their particular demands – despite the introduction of voluntary party quotes and reserved seats for women in some MENA parliaments.

Figure 5.7. **Male and female youth engagement in civic activities in MENA countries, 2012**

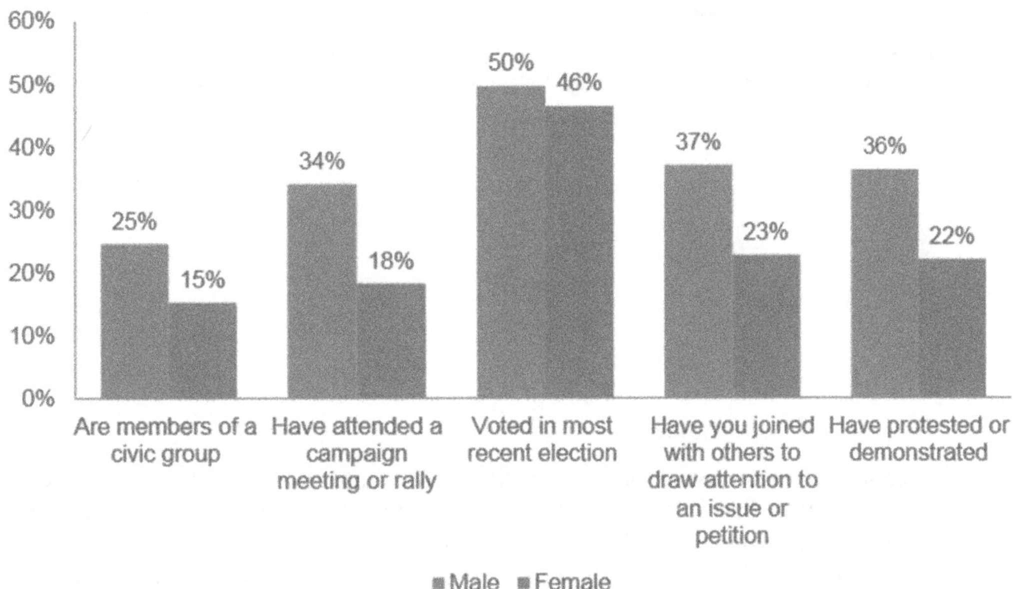

Source: Mercy Corps (2012), "Civic engagement of youth in the Middle East and North Africa: An analysis of key drivers and outcomes", March, http://www.mercycorps.org/sites/default/files/mena_youth_civic_engagement_study_-_final.pdf.

As discussed previously, the backlog in women's participation in economic and public life is also due to traditional gender norms and stereotypes that identify men as the main breadwinners. According to a study undertaken by the National Democratic Institute, a majority of men reported to be more comfortable working with a male boss because they could not accept taking orders from a woman (National Democratic Institute, 2012).

Recommendations

MENA governments can support young women in addressing the double challenge of gender-based barriers and those associated with their status as youth by:

1. **Undertaking a systematic review of the legislation to eliminate all forms of discrimination** in the legal system and ensure that international norms related to gender equality are fully embedded in the national legislative framework, especially those that affect the development of young women.
2. **Reviewing existing workplace regulation** with a view to eliminating provisions which discourage young women to apply and strengthening measures to facilitate women's economic participation (e.g. work-life measures).

3. **Integrating the specific needs of young women in national youth strategies and gender equality strategies** to mutually reinforce each other and empower young women in economic and public life.
4. **Gathering sex- and age-disaggregated data sets** to promote better informed policy-decisions, especially in the area of critical public services such as education, employment and health.
5. **Increasing the opportunities for young women and women associations** to participate in all spheres of public life including civic engagement, participation in youth-representative bodies and standing for leadership positions.

Notes

1. For more information, see www.oecd.org/gov/trust-in-government.htm.
2. "People's trust in institutions and in their own future is one of the most precious assets a country has: it is the cornerstone of effective governance, the main ingredient to promote economic growth and social progress." - OECD Secretary General, Joint Conference of OECD and Transparency International on the Link between Integrity and Regaining Young People's Trust, 9 December 2013, Paris.
3. Tunisia (79th), Morocco (80th) and Egypt (94th), Yemen (161th).
4. Based on data provided by the International Budget Partnership's Country Info, http://internationalbudget.org/opening-budgets/open-budget-initiative/open-budget-survey/country-info/.
5. For more information, see OECD work on youth, www.oecd.org/youth.htm.
6. In this report, informal employment refers to the total number of persons whose main job was informal. A job is informal when it lacks basic social or legal protections or employment benefits and may be found in the formal sector, informal sector or households (ILO, 2012).
7. Calculated on the basis of available data for Egypt, Jordan, Morocco, Palestinian Authority and Yemen.

References

Afiouni, Fida, Huub Ruël and Randall Schuler (2014), "HRM in the Middle East: Toward a greater understanding", *The International Journal of Human Resource Management*, 25:2, pp. 133-143, www.tandfonline.com/doi/pdf/10.1080/09585192.2013.826911 (accessed on 1 April 2016).

Ahmed, et al., (2012), *Youth Unemployment in the MENA Region: Determinants and Challenges*, IMF, Washington DC, www.imf.org/external/np/vc/2012/061312.htm (accessed on 1 April 2016).

Al Bawsala (2016), "Marsad Budget", http://budget.marsad.tn/fr/ (accessed on 2 April 2016).

Angel-Urdinola, Diego F. and Kimie Tanabe (2012), *Micro-Determinants of Informal Employment in the Middle East and North Africa Region*, World Bank, Washington, DC.

Association Tunisienne des Contrôleurs Publics (2015), *La petite corruption: Un danger banalisé - Étude exploratoire sur la perception de la petite corruption en Tunisie*, www.atcp.org.tn/petite_Corruption_Danger_Banalise_ATC_%202015.pdf (accessed on 1 April 2016).

Barsoum, Ghada, Mohamed Ramadan and Mona Mostafa (2014), "Labour market transitions of young women and men in Egypt", *Work4Youth Publication Series*, No. 16, June, ILO, Geneva.

Bergh, Sylvia I (2014), "Decentralisation and local governance in the MENA region", www.tunisia.unisi.it/wp-content/uploads/sites/5/2014/07/Art.-Bergh.pdf.

City of Boston (n.d.), "Youth Lead the Change: Participatory Budgeting Boston", Division of Youth Engagement and Employment, http://youth.boston.gov/youth-lead-the-change/ (accessed on 12 April 2016).

Council of Europe (2013), "Revised European Charter on the Participation of Young People in Local and Regional Life", www.coe.int/t/dg4/youth/Source/Resources/PR_material/2015_Brochure_Youth_Participation_Charter_web_ENG.pdf (accessed on 1 April 2016).

European Commission (2015), "Better Regulation Toolbox", http://ec.europa.eu/smart-regulation/guidelines/docs/br_toolbox_en.pdf (accessed on 12 April 2016).

European Youth Capital (2016), "About", www.europeanyouthcapital.org/about/ (accessed on 12 April 2016).

Freund, Caroline and Bob Rijkers (2012), “Employment miracles”, paper presented at the 13th Jacques Polak Annual Research Conference, hosted by the International Monetary Fund, Washington, DC, 8-9 November, www.imf.org/external/np/res/seminars/2012/arc/pdf/FR.pdf (accessed on 1 April 2016).

Gilman, Hollie Russon (2014), “What happened when the City of Boston asked teenagers for help with the budget”, 26 June, https://nextcity.org/daily/entry/boston-young-people-participatory-budgeting-winners-youth-lead-change (accessed on 1 April 2016).

Government of Hong Kong (n.d.), www.budget.gov.hk/2010/chi/flip/main.html (accessed on 12 April 2016).

ILO (International Labour Organization) (2012), “Statistical update on employment in the informal economy”, Department of Statistics, June, http://laborsta.ilo.org/informal_economy_E.html (accessed on 1 April 2016).

Independent Commission against Corruption of Hong Kong (n.d.), ïTeen Camp”, www.iteencamp.icac.hk/EngIntro/Shows (accessed on 12 April 2016).

International Budget Partnership (n.d.), “Results by country”, http://internationalbudget.org/opening-budgets/open-budget-initiative/open-budget-survey/country-info/ (accessed on 1 April 2016).

Koordinatti (n.d.), “Development Centre of Youth Information and Counselling”, www.koordinaatti.fi/sites/default/files/koordinaatti-and-initiative-channel.pdf (accessed on 10 April 2016).

Mercy Corps (2012), “Civic engagement of youth in the Middle East and North Africa: An analysis of key drivers and outcomes”, March, www.mercycorps.org/sites/default/files/mena_youth_civic_engagement_study_-_final.pdf (accessed on 1 April 2016).

Naser, Teycir Ben (2014), *La démocratie participative : et si les municipalités s'y mettaient vraiment?*, 17 November, http://nawaat.org/portail/2014/11/17/la-democratie-participative-et-si-les-municipalites-sy-mettaient-vraiment/ (accessed on 1 April 2016).

National Democratic Institute (2012), “Women's Political Participation in Tunisia after the Revolution. Findings From Focus Groups in Tunisia”, www.ndi.org/files/womens-political-participation-Tunisia-FG-2012-ENG.pdf (accessed on 1 April 2016).

Nuortenideat (2016), https://www.nuortenideat.fi/fi/ (accessed on 10 April 2016).

Observatoire National de l'Emploi et des Qualifications (2014), “Transition vers le marché du travail des jeunes femmes et hommes en Tunisie”, *Work4Youth Publication Series*, No. 15, June, ILO, Geneva.

Observatoire National de la Jeunesse (n.d.), “Projet AGORA débat de la ville”, www.onj.nat.tn/index.php/fr/projets/projet-agora-debat-de-la-ville (accessed on 1 April 2016).

OECD (forthcoming), “Towards better public governance : Performance-based budgeting”.

OECD (2015), "Tackling youth unemployment in the MENA region", key findings in the presentation, www.oecd.org/mena/investment/PPT_website.pdf (accessed on 1 April 2016).

OECD (2013a), "Strengthening Fiscal Transparency for Better Public Governance in Tunisia", www.oecd.org/gov/budgeting/T4%20-MENA%20SBO%202013%20-%20documents%20Session%201.pdf.

OECD (2013b), *Regulatory Reform in the Middle East and North Africa: Implementing Regulatory Policy Principles to Foster Inclusive Growth*, OECD Publishing, Paris, http://dx.doi.org/10.1787/9789264204553-en.

OECD (2013c), *OECD e-Government Studies: Egypt 2012*, OECD Publishing, Paris, http://dx.doi.org/10.1787/9789264178786-en.

OECD (2012), "Recommendation of the Council on Regulatory Policy and Governance", www.oecd.org/governance/regulatory-policy/49990817.pdf (accessed on 1 April 2016).

OECD (2009), "Regional Charter for Regulatory Quality", www.oecd.org/mena/governance/45187832.pdf.

OECD (n.d.a), "Trust in government", www.oecd.org/gov/trust-in-government.htm (accessed on 1 April 2016).

OECD (n.d.b), "OECD work on youth", www.oecd.org/youth.htm (accessed on 1 April 2016).

OECD/CAWTAR (2014), *Women in Public Life: Gender, Law and Policy in the Middle East and North Africa*, OECD Publishing, Paris, http://dx.doi.org/10.1787/9789264224636-en.

OECD CleanGovBiz (2013), "Integrity scan of Tunisia", www.oecd.org/cleangovbiz/Tunisia-Integrity-ScanEN.pdf.

Open Government Partnership (2015), Finland Open Government Action Plan 2015-2017, www.opengovpartnership.org/sites/default/files/OGP_Action_Plan_Finland-2015_2017.pdf (accessed on 1 April 2016).

Open Government Partnership (n.d.), "Jordan", www.opengovpartnership.org/country/jordan/action-plan (accessed on 1 April 2016).

O'Sullivan, Anthony, Marie-Estelle Rey and Jorge Galvez Mendey (2013), "Opportunities and challenges in the MENA region", www.oecd.org/mena/competitiveness/49036903.pdf (accessed on 1 April 2016).

Rabbaa, Nadia (2015), "Mustapha El Mnasfi: 'Au Maroc, on exclut les jeunes des décisions'", *Jeune Afrique*, www.jeuneafrique.com/mag/252810/politique/mustapha-el-mnasfi-au-maroc-on-exclut-les-jeunes-des-decisions/ (accessed on 1 April 2016).

Refstie, Hilde (2012), "Youth: The face of urbanisation", *Sharing Knowledge and Learning from Cities (CIVIS)*, No. 6, January, www.academia.edu/27700047/Youth_the_face_of_urbanization (accessed on 1 April 2016).

Schauer, Katrin and Susanne Klinzing (2012), "Selected international good practices in youth participation at the local level", IJAB and Fachstelle für Internationale Jugendarbeit der Bundesrepublik Deutschland e.V., www.ijab.de/uploads/tx_ttproducts/datasheet/Youth_Participation_at_local_level.pdf (accessed on 1 April 2016).

Swedish International Development Cooperation Agency (2012), "Public financial management for the rights of children and young people", www.sida.se/contentassets/dfa19bd6efc84f25800edaa90590008e/public-financial-management-for-the-rights-of-children-and-young-people_3224.pdf (accessed on 1 April 2016).

Transparency International (2014a), *Corruption Perceptions Index 2014*, www.transparency.org/cpi2014/results (accessed on 10 April 2016).

Transparency International (2014b), "Anti-corruption kit: 15 ideas for young activists", http://issuu.com/transparencyinternational/docs/2014_anticorruptionkit_youth__en?e=2496456/8912943 (accessed on 2 April 2016).

UN Habitat (2012), *The State of Arab Cities 2012 - Challenges of Urban Transition*, Regional Cities Reports, http://unhabitat.org/books/the-state-of-arab-cities-2012-challenges-of-urban-transition/ (accessed on 1 April 2016).

United Cities and Local Governments (2013), "Executive summary", *Basic Services for All in an Urbanizing World*, Third Global Report on Local Democracy and Decentralization GOLD III, www.uclg.org/sites/default/files/re_gold_eng.pdf (accessed on 1 April 2016).

Wally, Nermine (2012), "Youth, skills and productive work analysis report on the Middle East and North Africa region", background paper, *Education for All Global Monitoring Report*, UNESCO, http://unesdoc.unesco.org/images/0021/002185/218523e.pdf (accessed on 1 April 2016).

World Bank (2014), *Economy Rankings database*, Doing Business - Measuring Business Regulations, www.doingbusiness.org/rankings (accessed on 1 April 2016).

World Bank (2013), *Women, Business and the Law 2014: Removing Restrictions to Enhance Gender Equality*, World Bank, Washington DC, http://wbl.worldbank.org/~/media/WBG/WBL/Documents/Reports/2014/Women-Business-and-the-Law-2014-Key-Findings.pdf?la=en (accessed on 1 April 2016).

World Bank (2005), "Egypt Public Expenditure Review", Policy Note 7, *Capital investment in the education sector*, www.mof.gov.eg/MOFGallerySource/English/policy-notes/Egypt%20PER-SchoolBuilding%20(7).pdf (accessed on 1 April 2016).

World Bank (n.d.a), *Workforce database*, Enterprise Surveys, www.enterprisesurveys.org/data/exploretopics/workforce#--7 (accessed on 1 April 2016).

World Bank (n.d.b), *Women, Business and the Law database*, Data. Going to Court. http://wbl.worldbank.org/data/exploretopics/going-to-court#judicial-representation (accessed on 1 April 2016).

World Bank (n.d.c), "Population in the largest city (% of urban population)", World Bank Data, http://data.worldbank.org/indicator/EN.URB.LCTY.UR.ZS/countries (accessed on 1 April 2016).

World Bank (n.d.d), "Urban population (% of total)", World Bank Data, http://data.worldbank.org/indicator/SP.URB.TOTL.IN.ZS.

ORGANISATION FOR ECONOMIC CO-OPERATION AND DEVELOPMENT

The OECD is a unique forum where governments work together to address the economic, social and environmental challenges of globalisation. The OECD is also at the forefront of efforts to understand and to help governments respond to new developments and concerns, such as corporate governance, the information economy and the challenges of an ageing population. The Organisation provides a setting where governments can compare policy experiences, seek answers to common problems, identify good practice and work to co-ordinate domestic and international policies.

The OECD member countries are: Australia, Austria, Belgium, Canada, Chile, the Czech Republic, Denmark, Estonia, Finland, France, Germany, Greece, Hungary, Iceland, Ireland, Israel, Italy, Japan, Korea, Latvia, Luxembourg, Mexico, the Netherlands, New Zealand, Norway, Poland, Portugal, the Slovak Republic, Slovenia, Spain, Sweden, Switzerland, Turkey, the United Kingdom and the United States. The European Union takes part in the work of the OECD.

OECD Publishing disseminates widely the results of the Organisation's statistics gathering and research on economic, social and environmental issues, as well as the conventions, guidelines and standards agreed by its members.

OECD PUBLISHING, 2, rue André-Pascal, 75775 PARIS CEDEX 16
(42 2016 35 1 P) ISBN 978-92-64-26573-8 – 2016

www.ingramcontent.com/pod-product-compliance
Lightning Source LLC
LaVergne TN
LVHW081411110826
845149LV00010B/1703

* 9 7 8 9 2 6 4 2 6 5 7 3 8 *